Jacqueline's Journey

By

Yvonne Bloor

Copyright © 2025 Jacqueline's Journey

ISBN: 978-1-917601-97-9

All rights reserved, including the right to reproduce this book, or portions thereof in any form. No part of this text may be reproduced, transmitted, downloaded, decompiled, reverse engineered, or stored, in any form or introduced into any information storage and retrieval system, in any form or by any means, whether electronic or mechanical without the express written permission of the author.

This is a work of fiction. Names and characters are the product of the author's imagination and any resemblance to actual persons, living or dead, is entirely coincidental.

ACKOWLEDGEMENTS

I am so grateful to my dear friend June who has creatively assisted me with the aspects of arts and crafts within the book. Thank you, best bud, for inspiring me.

I wish to say a big Thank you to my dear friend Leonora for her encouragement and support throughout my writing of this book.

Moreover, I would like to mention Boldon Community Library and Shields Radio Station for their interest in my book. Thank you for inviting me to come along and talk about it.

My dear beautiful daughter Sarah and lovely son in law Keith deserve a mention, who have always been supportive of my writing. Thank you for being there.

Finally, a big Thank you to my sister Sandra and my brother Colin who have always believed in my work. And, to my readers. I hope this one is as enjoyable to you as it was for me to write it.

Yvonne Bloor

Chapter 1

It was a quiet evening for Jacqueline as the children were all grown up now and were busy with their own lives. Niamh was now in her last year at university, and didn't she know it! There was little time to socialise. She was energised by the fact that her degree was coming to an end, and she could spend some time with the family at home. She missed her sister and her cheeky brother Colm.

Colm was sitting back in the armchair, laid back as always, with his glass of beer. He congratulated his sister Emily on her forthcoming marriage as he kissed her cheek. He was now nineteen years old and still as relaxed as he ever as he made a little speech.

'To my sister, who will be moving on to pastures new. Good luck to you and Frankie, he is a good lad that one', as he gave a sly wink towards Frankie.

Emily quickly responded with a direct answer.

'Not so fast Colm! Are you trying to get rid of me?

'Me, Nah! Sis, just giving you a push like', as he moved towards Emily and whispered

'Just kidding Sis'.

Emily and Frankie left to meet up with friends at the local pub. Niamh got back to her studying and Colm went to lay down in his bedroom with his newspaper in his hand.

Jacqueline sat by the fire watching the flames glowing, she could feel that slight breeze as the northeast wind was whistling away down the chimney breast, it was a soothing sound she thought. She began to reminisce about the evening she spent with Declan when they first moved into the cosy mining cottage overlooking Trow Rocks.

Declan carried her over the threshold, and they slept by the fire on their first night.

'How long ago was that' she said to herself, 'it must be twenty-five years.'

She sat on the floor going through all the photographs of when they first met, there were so many, as Jacqueline loved to get her dad's old camera out at every opportunity.

'Why couldn't I have had another twenty-five years with Declan!' As she looked across at the wooden mounted cross of Our Lord which was hanging in the corner alcove. Jacqueline stared at the cross with a scornful look for some time and the tears began to flow. She looked up and asked the question,

'What do you have in store for me then for the rest of my life, what! I am lost at sea, you do know that don't you', as she was expecting a reply, but she knew it would never come.

She became emotional and started to gather up all the photographs and suddenly realised when she caught a glimpse of the photograph in her hand, it was that of her three children. Her heart wretched wide open as she shouted out!

'I am sorry, I am sorry, I am blessed, yes, I am blessed' as she knelt and looked over to the wooden cross of our Lord.

'I know it's been eighteen months since Declan passed, but it seems like yesterday'. Jaqueline gathered her thoughts and jumped up off the floor and quickly put the photographs back in the drawer at the bottom of the bureau.

'I need a walk, I need the sea and sand, that's what I need'. She put on her brown duffle coat and woolly brown hat and beige scarf. As she opened the back door, the wind caught the side of her cheek.

'Oh, it's like that is it, a blasting wind that numbs the teeth.

'Aw well, I do need a wakeup call I think' she muttered to herself.

Jacqueline made her way down to the beach, pulled her hat over her ears, and grabbed her hood up from her duffle coat to keep the chill off her. The side of her ears and face were now frozen.

She walked briskly towards the Disappearing Gun; there were quite a few walkways that were breathtaking with the silky sand blowing in the wind and the rocks looked like they were shivering away. Jacqueline gave out a wry smile, it didn't matter to her that the wind was vicious, as the walk was inspiring, it was the view from the hilltop that embraced her soul. The captivating portrait of the lashing waves and the sunset just showing its face.

The sky began to colour with that reddish sultry ambience of a warming sense of comfort.

'I feel a poem coming on' she said to herself. 'Just as well I brought a notebook and pen with me'.

Sunset :
The Clouds come a light
The essence such red and bright..
For the atmosphere lifts with a glow
As the smoky clouds fold up and bring
On the richness of a beautiful red bow
The wind comes alive and swaggers with pride
For there is nothing but nature to swallow and smother the outside
Sunset the inspiration of light for there is nothing to affright...

Jacqueline sat between the rocks in her usual alcove and felt at peace, peace within herself and peace with God. She realised that nature does work in mysterious ways.

'Oh goodness, I have lost track of time again! It's six o'clock! She ran up the hill and into the cottage. Colm heard the back door, and made his way to the kitchen and shouted,

'Is that you mam?' Colm shouted out.

'Yes, it's me son', as Jacqueline turned towards him.

Colm quickly moved towards his mam.

'Where have you been mam, I was getting a bit worried to be honest'.

'I went for a walk and lost track of time'.

'You and your walks mam, you will catch your death one of these days'. Colm spoke with relief in his voice.

'It's too glorious out their son to catch your death'. They both smiled at one another.

'Fish and Chips mam?' 'You read my mind son'. Colm got into his car, any opportunity to go out in the car, as he had recently passed his test and inherited his dad's car. Jacqueline was pleased that she could have some quality time with her son. He was a good thoughtful lad.

Colm had bought himself an extra portion of chips, as he was starving. It had been a busy day at the shipyard. He was becoming a first-class draughtsman, following in his father's footsteps. He was ready for his big fish supper.

'You should start the book club again, you loved it so much mam', said he.

Jacqueline quickly reciprocated with a puzzled look,

'I passed that on to Lydia son, I told you that ages ago...,' said she

'So, what you got planned mam, I see you still writing your poetry', why don't you go to college mam and see what is on offer?'.

Jacqueline was stunned by Colm's remark!

'It makes sense mam, doing what you love best'. She sat back in the chair and glanced back at Colm with a surprised look on her face.

'I think I am bit too old for that now son'.

'You are never too old mam, I know there are some men in the office that have studied in their forties, let's face it mam you are only forty-three, think about it will you?'

Jacqueline gave her son a thoughtful look, 'You are a good lad no mistake, I will think about it promise'.

The telephone rang, it was Niamh, Colm answered the telephone, and Niamh replied with an energetic tone in her voice.

'Hiya bro, what you up to then, I thought you would be out galivanting...'.

'Cheeky! I just been having a fish supper with me mam'. Said Colm

'Oh, get you then'. Replied Niamh.

'How's Uni, are you doing ok sis?'.

Niamh replied with a hopeful expression on her face.

'Yes, it's getting harder in my last year, but I am enjoying it, I think I will apply for a teaching post once I have finished'.

'Wow sis, that would fab, so happy for you'.

'How's mam Colm?'. 'She is doing ok; I have just been trying to persuade her to go back to college'.

'I think that's a great idea Colm, put her on!'. '

Jacqueline quickly made her way to the telephone and replied energetically.

Hello pet, how are you?'

Niamh was smiling down the telephone at this point and answered her mam with a warm tone in her voice.

'I am fine mam, but you really need to think about going down to the college and seeing what is on offer, I am sure they will have something that you would love'. I am coming home for a few days.

'That's wonderful pet, you haven't been home for ages, said Jacqueline.

'I have been working flat out on my dissertation, and I need some sea air for a change; we can go to the college together mam'. Niamh was determined to get her mam to college.

'I see, I am ambushed by the pair of you by the looks of it!'

They both laughed out loudly,

'So it's settled then mam?'

'Yes, if you say so pet'.

Colm put his arm around his mam as he moved towards the front door,

'Right mam, I am off downtown with the lads, see you later'.

Jacqueline gave her son a hug and made her way into the living room to digest what had just occurred. She sat in the chair for a good while contemplating. This bizarre idea of me going to college.

'Could I really do this, perhaps I should look for a day course at first, maybe', as she tried to think it through in her mind. It took over all her thoughts that night and took her back to when she left school and was thinking so much about college and then she met Declan and her whole life changed.

'Perhaps I need this change'. I have given up the Book Club, so why not?'. Jacqueline had tired herself out that night and fell into bed and slept until six the next morning.

Niamh arrived early; she let herself in with her key.

'I am home mam, you ready for your day out at the college mam'.

Jacqueline came down the stairs,

'You're an early bird'. Said she

'I thought we would make a day of it mam and go to town have some lunch, what do you think?'

'Aw that would be nice pet, just let me get my shoes on and we can be off, you had your breakfast mind'.

'Yes, mam, I am all grown up now', as they both hugged and smiled at each other. Jacqueline gave her daughter a peck on the cheek.

'What's that for mam'. As Niamh looked surprised.

'It's for you being wonderful you, that's what that is for', as Jacqueline gave her daughter a loving smile.

They both made their way to the bus stop,

'Once I am finished at Uni mam, I am going to sort out some driving lessons. Said Niamh

Jacqueline responded with a coy gesture.

'Yes, I would imagine you would, I don't mind the bus rides, I like the scenery'.

Niamh gave her mam an odd look, 'Really mam'.

'Yes, really'.as Jacqueline raised her eyebrows.

The bus stopped outside Deeside College, which was adjacent to Deeside University, just off Brampton Road. As they strolled through the grounds. Niamh made the comment of how oldy worldly the building looked, it was a carbon copy of the university.

'I wonder if it was partitioned off in the past to make way for diplomas' thought Niamh…

Jacqueline was more interested in the landscape that surrounded it, with all those trees and configurations of planted flowers that were arranged in a symmetrical fashion. She was mesmerised by it all…

They both made their way to the reception area and the receptionist was very friendly and helpful. She outlined the syllabus, and there were quite a few classes that consisted of literature and language, and there was also a day course of writing and poetry.

Jacqueline was taken with the day course, every Friday for 6 months, but Niamh felt that she could tackle the full course of literature and language if she pushed herself. It was decided they would take all the literature with them and have a good discussion over lunch at the Seabowl in town; the new restaurant that had just opened, as Niamh was keen to check it out.

As they entered the restaurant, Jacqueline couldn't help but notice the vintage décor, its 50s style look which was so quaint.

'I hope the food isn't vintage mam?' As Niamh looked on in astonishment.

The waitresses were dressed in black dresses with white caps and aprons, and white sleeved cuffs. Jacqueline loved it. They were playing Glen Miller music. The atmosphere was euphoric. It was very busy, but they managed to get a table in the corner. The table was decorated with beige tablecloths, a white flowery vase with lovely carnations in them. The menu was mounted in a rack, and it was well presented.

There were bacon and brie sandwiches, hot roasted sandwiches, with salad dressings or roast potatoes. The pasta dishes were to Niamh's liking, they had a special sauce which was not identified in the menu.

Niamh was intrigued she was sticking with that. Jacqueline was taken with the hot roast pork sandwiches with roast potatoes. She felt famished suddenly which was unusual for her as she wasn't eating that well these days, the grieving process of losing her husband still hadn't left her and her appetite fluctuated from day to day.

Niamh's pasta had arrived, and it didn't disappoint it was meatballs, cheesy pasta with a gorgeous sauce it tasted like plums and cherries, she hadn't tasted anything like that before. Jacqueline's hot roast melted in her mouth.

Once they had finished their lovely meal Niamh got out the literature and explained to her mam in a persuasive manner that the literature class covered all aspect of literature and poetry, and, it had her mam's favourite writers and poets.

Jacqueline was so animated and had not felt that feeling for a long time; it was decided that they both would go back the next day, and Jacqueline would sign up for the literature and language course at the University that would start in September.

Niamh pointed out to her mam that she could do a summer school short course at the college before she started university and that would give her more confidence.

'You have thought of everything my pet' as Jacqueline replied, I think you will make an excellent teacher our Niamh'.

'Right mam time for a celebration, let's go to the bistro bar and have a glass of wine, it's a celebration'. Jacqueline couldn't believe the day she was having, 'I will have to pinch myself when I get home, is this really me'.

The next day ended up with Jacqueline signing up to the summer school courses at the college to get her into university. She walked out of the college with Niamh and felt a strange feeling in the back of her neck, a touch, like it was Declan passing through, giving her a loving hug. She couldn't get over that strange moment that night, it stayed with her. This calming sensation of something? She didn't know what, a new adventure beckoned towards her for some reason. She lay on top of the bed and quietly drifted in a soothing sleep. Her journey had just begun…

Chapter 2

The dawn came quickly, as Emily was the first to surface on this Wednesday morning in late January, it was a fresh cold one, as the frost had settled across the garden fence. As Emily looked out of the bedroom window, she caught a glimpse of the misted spray that was gliding across the sea, moving so swiftly; a vision that captures your imagination, almost like ghosts gliding on the waves, such shapes and forms that glide in and out in their symmetrical formation. She was startled by the vision and could not take her eyes of the ghostly shapes that waved in and out.

'I have never seen such a formation before, you would think they were ghost like figures dancing on the waves' Emily shook herself, 'I sound like mam', as she moved away from the window and headed to the bathroom to get washed and ready for the day.

It was going to be a big day, as Emily was expanding the wool shop, and the next-door renovations were taking place this very day. The Wool shop was extending his habitat to hand-made jewellery made from the beach stones that lay around the beach. Belinda her assistant had become an asset, as she had a flare for making things out of nothing. There was also going to be various ornaments made from beach stones. Young Jenny was the junior assistant who was fitting in nicely with the staff.

'I better get a move on; the deliveries and workmen will be banging on the door'. Aunt Aileen didn't disappoint as she was knocking on the Gibson's door to pick up Emily. Colm answered the door as he left for work with his usual toast in his mouth, nothing ever changes with Colm.

'Hi Aunt Aileen, mam's just getting up, she must have had a lie in. Emily is banging about upstairs; she must be about ready, 'see you later'.

Emily came dashing down the stairs, 'Am I late! 'No, it's me I am bright and early, take your time, have a cup of tea and piece of toast, we have got twenty minutes or so to kill before the deliveries arrive'. Emily gave out a pleasing sigh, 'Thank you! I need a cup'.

'Is your mam ok Emily'. 'I think so, I was late coming in last night I was at Frankies'. Jacqueline strolled down the stairs, bleary eyed, she hadn't slept well. She kept waking up every hour with mixed and confused thoughts of her future and she couldn't get Declan's presence out of her mind, it was as if he was in the room. She couldn't understand it, as she hadn't had those feelings for some months now.

Aileen went over to her sister, 'Hey sis, you look tired, are you ok?'. 'Yes, I think so, have you time today to have a good catch up. 'Just let me drop Emily off, I will be back, get the kettle on ready'. Jacqueline gave her sister a hug and went upstairs to wash and dress.

It was not long before Aileen was back, and they both sat in the kitchen and had a good talk about the last two days Jacqueline had spent with Niamh. Aileen was shocked, surprised, but very pleased that Jacqueline had taken further steps to conquer her grief and loss of Delcan. 'Does Sara know your plans yet. 'No, I have not had chance to get used to them myself'. As Jacqueline laughed out loud, nervously, I will call her later, I think she is on shift at the hospital until 3pm'.

'Why don't we all go out tonight, the three of us, we have not done that in ages.' Jacqueline gave her sister a mischievous look, 'That sounds inviting, let's do it, I will call Sara later. We can just walk along to the Sand View'. Aileen responded by saying, 'Oh yes, we have not been in there, I am sure we haven't'.

Jacqueline gazed at her sister with a heartfelt expression. 'It was Declan's favourite place to eat'. Aileen looked on with a reserved gaze, 'Are you sure you want to'. They both stared at one another and Jacqueline announced loudly! 'I feel the need to for some reason, I don't know why'

'I think maybe Delcan's spiritual presence is having an effect on you, it's not a bad thing, as you are being so calm about it, which is good'. They held each other's hand and poured out a further cup of tea.

'Oh Aileen, I am so nervous about going back to school, our Niamh makes it look so right, and I feel confident when she is around, but last night I just couldn't get to sleep'.

'Let me ask you, are you excited about it, does it fill you with joy'. Jacqueline's eyes lit up, 'Yes! My goodness! yes!

'There you are then, all settled, your nerves and butterflies will flit away once you have gotten over your first day, for heaven's sake, you ran the Book Club, that was a challenge girl!

'Oh yes! With a smirky expression on her face, it was indeed!

'Oh, our Aileen, you have made me feel so much better already'.

'I am off I will see you at 7pm, bye pet'.

Jacqueline felt a sense of ease about her as she went about completing her daily chores, washing, ironing, and hoovering through the house. She had put the radio on and was happy to listen along to some symphony music on radio three, as she found this music so serene. She particularly liked the clarinet and violin.

'How talented they are so dedicated to their graft', as she muttered and hummed to herself'.

The doorbell rang, and Jacqueline turned down the music as she opened the door, she was so surprised to see Serena, they hadn't seen each other much since the wedding.

'Hello Serena, what a lovely surprise, come in'. Serena looked radiant and glowing like a beacon. 'I wanted to come and tell you about the good news in person'. 'That's sound ominous, I will pop the kettle on, and you can tell me your good news', as Jacqueline waited with bated breath!

'I am just so excited Jacqueline! I going to have a baby!'. Jacqueline stepped backwards and clutched the kitchen door, 'Oh how fabulous! Serena, I am so happy for you and Dylan, I really am.

Serena turned to Jacqueline, 'I just wish Declan was here to see his brother become a father'. Jacqueline gave her a heartened look, 'He is here in spirit Jacqeline, and I know he would have been over the moon for you and Dylan'.

'How far along are you?'. 'I am 4 months'

'No milk for me Jacqueline, I keep having morning sickness when I drink milk at the moment'. 'Yes, certain things trigger off morning sickness, but it will pass.'

'Oh, it's not too bad, it's just now and then'.

'Your parents must be over the moon.'

'Mum is already ordering things, I have told her not to, not just yet it's too early, she gets carried away with it all, Dad just beams and lets her get on with it'.

'I have some news too; I am going back to school'.

Serena grasped Jacqueline's hand, 'Oh Jacqueline that is good news, you will love it, you really will'.

Jacqueline was beginning to think more and more about this and realising she might just love it; she was getting more convinced by the minute. Serena and Jacqueline spent some time chatting and Serena's confident manner was rubbing off on Jacqueline.

'You can come round more often girl; you are giving me that boost of confidence I really need'.

Serena put her arm around Jacqueline, 'You just have to believe in yourself, and rest will take care of itself, it's a known fact, trust me I know, I am Solicitor'.

Jacqueline had this enormous, big grin on her face, 'Of course, if you cannot trust a Solicitor, then who can you trust'. They both laughed and hugged each other.

'This has been lovely afternoon, you come back soon Serena', as Jacqueline walked Serena to the door.

Time was getting on and Jacqueline continued to wash up and prepare for tea.

'Oh, my goodness!' it's four thirty, how time flies when you are having fun'. Jacqueline put the radio back on and sang along as she peeled the potatoes and vegetables. There was half a beef joint left from Sunday.

'Colm loves his dinners, Jacqueline smiled to herself'.

As the door opened, Colm walked in and shouted up,

'Oh mam, I can smell that delicious food, it's roast beef dinner isn't it'.

'It is that you son, you get washed up and it will be on the table in fifteen minutes, Emily should be home by then'.

No sooner had Jacqueline said that Emily walked through the door, 'That smells gorgeous mam'.

They all sat around the table and Jacqueline told them both the good news.

Colm looked across at his mam,

'I know mam Dylan told me at work. I knew Serena was coming around, so I kept that to myself'.

Emily was elated for Dylan and Serena. Jacqueline turned to Emily.

'I have not had a chance to tell you Emily of my news as you were out with Frankie last night, I am going back to school'

Emily jumped up and hugged her mam.

'Aww mam, that is such good news, you will be amazing, because you are amazing'.

Jacqueline started to well up with tears in her eyes.

Colm jumped up, 'Aww man, don't start that up, you will get me started, behave yourselves the pair of you.

They all hugged together and sat for a while chatting away. Colm began by saying that he was going to be promoted as he had completed the drawings on a new ship that was coming in drydock, 'The Mantrel'. The Manager was so impressed he has stepped him up from the junior level to a more senior position.

Jacqueline kissed her son, 'Congratulations son, your dad would have been so proud of you lad'.

'And to think mam, I told dad that I would not like it in the office'.

'Yes, well your dad always knew best, and he was always right'.

Emily joined in the conversation, 'I have some good news to share too, the new renovations are almost finished, and I will have to advertise for two more assistants, we are going to need them'.

Jacqueline asked her daughter if she was coping with all responsibilities given that her Aunt Aileen had now signed the shops over to her completely.

'I am coping well mam, my asthma hasn't affecting me over the years as you know mam, and it's a big boost of capital because Frankie and I have set a date for the wedding mam, and it is 12th May mam, put that in your calendar; and Colm, you are walking me down the aisle'.

Colm looked dumbfounded; Jacqueline was one happy mam.

'I have contacted Fr Donnelly to make sure he was free, and he is. The reception will be at the Pavilion, as it is so special to Frankie and me; that was our first dance together, on our third date. It's been renovated now into a venue for weddings, christening, and any other special occasion; Frankie and I went along the other night when I was so late getting in. Mam, it's amazing it just our special place.'

Jacqueline couldn't be happier, but how she so wished Declan was here to see all this, she felt that ghostly brush on her neck again as she got up from the table.

Her thoughts began to filter, 'It's Declan and his spirit, I do feel his spirit, if it's my imagination, then I gladly accept it because it feels real, a nice real I do not want to let go of.'

Jacqueline and Emily washed the dishes together and Colm went upstairs to get ready for his night out. Uncle Dylan was taking him for a celebration drink in honour of his promotion.

Emily turned to her mam,

'You are my inspiration mam, because you made me believe in myself, you just think on that and you believe in yourself now mam, it's your turn to shine'.

Jacqueline put her hands around her daughter's face and spoke so gently, 'You are really something, a shining star', I am blessed to have borne such wonderful children, and I thank God every day for that'.

Emily replied, 'That's enough of this admiration, I am off to get changed, Frankie and I going to the pictures, to watch that new adventure movie showing at the Paramount'

'Yes, I am going out with my sisters in a little while myself' as Jacqueline turned to Emily.

'Oh, you are, get you, dress up for a change mam, you should'.

Jacqueline smirked at her daughter, 'Hey you, I always look presentable when I go out'.

'I know you do but wear some bright colours for change'.

'I like black and navy blue'.

'You have got a lovely floral dress in the wardrobe mam, it's only seen the light of day, twice I bet'.

Jacqueline looked amazed as she knew Emily was right and she would give it some thought.

The night was going to be wonderful night for all the Gibsons, some joy had come into the house which had not been there for some time.

Chapter 3

Sara and Aileen had arrived at the cottage in a Taxi. It was Sara who jumped out of the taxi first, as she ran down the path to Jacquelines and knocked firmly on the door!

Jacqueline came rushing to the door and took one look at Sara with sarcastic response.

'That was some knock our Sara, bray the door down lass, why don't you! As they both laughed away.

'Come on then! our Jacqueline, get a move on girl, the table is booked for 7.30 pm'.

Jacqueline noticed how pale her sister Sara was looking.

'Are you alright our Sara?'

Sara turned to Jacqueline, 'I will tell you all about it when we get in the restaurant, I am in need of a glass of wine'.

Jacqueline looked a little alarmed, as she knew her sister well, and she liked a glass of wine now and then, but she was never in need of one.

As they all entered the restaurant and ordered their food and drink. Sara began to tell what was on her mind.

'I think John is seeing someone again, it is happening again! I am sure of it. He has been working in Glasgow; he tells me he is drumming up more business and has some good contacts and he needs to stay over to complete the deal'.

Aileen began to respond first by saying, 'I cannot believe that is true Sara, I think you worrying too much about nothing, I know he has cheated on you before, but that was ages ago, and he has been devoted to you since then'.

Sara frantically replied,

'We don't need more business Aileen we just don't, I am not convinced at all this time!'

Jacqueline suggested that they had a day out in Glasgow and perhaps do a spot of sleuthing as she turned to Sara.

'Do you know where John is staying in Glasgow Sara?'.

'Yes, as a matter of fact I do know where he is staying, at the Chorlton'.

Jacqueline remembered that the Criton was very near the Chorlton Hotel,

She glanced at Sara and spoke convincingly.

'Aww the Criton is just down the road, why don't we book in there for a night, and see what John is up to'?

Sara looked at Jacqueline.

'Really, are you kidding me, we cannot do that surely'.

Jacqueline pointed out that Sara needed to get some peace of mind, and what a good way to put her mind at ease one way or another.

Aileen and Jacqueline hounded Sara until she gave in and said,

'Ok at least I will know where I stand, there is that I suppose', as Sara looked on with a worrying look.

They would all book in the hotel the very next night.

Sara went on to say that John was going to the business centre in town. Aileen reacted by saying,

'We will have to be inconspicuous; I think we need to set a plan of action'. What do you have in mind our Aileen, as Jacqueline looked rather intrigued. Aileen went on to say,

'The business centre is a venue where my Arthur attends twice a year; we can mingle inconspicuously, but if we do happen to bump into John, I could explain that I am there in place of my Arthur and you two came along for a shopping spree' Sarah smiled, 'that's sounds feasible'.

The three sisters looked at one another and made a pact putting one hand on each other, as they said together,

'Tomorrow then, raise your glasses girls'.

'Here is to amateur sleuthing'…

The conversation turned to some good news as Jacqueline let her sisters know of a happy event.

'There is going to be a birth, Serena is pregnant'.

Aileen and Sara were so happy for Serena and Dylan, and went on to say,

'I am happy not having children, love them, but love giving them back' as they both laughed together.

Jacqueline responded with her view on the matter,

'I was truly blessed with my three beautiful children'.

Aileen looked at Jacqueline, 'You were born to have children, as you always looked out for Sara and me, you are the most caring and thoughtful of us all our Jacqueline'.

'It's time we should be heading home as Jacqueline give out a little yawn'.

Sara agreed as she too was little tired, they made their way to taxi rank and kissed one another good night.

'Until tomorrow sisters, as Jacqueline waved them off'.

She entered the front door of her cottage; her thoughts were of Declan and how lucky she had been never to have had any worries or fears where Declan was concerned. She sat on the settee with a cup of tea in hand,

'Let's hope this trip ends on a good note and Sara's fears disappear and John is just working hard on a deal?'

Colm entered the living room', Jacqueline turned her head,

'Hello Son, good night out'. '

'Actually mam, guess who I bumped into at the Zion bistro, no other than Bernadette'. Said he

Jacqueline gave her son a pleasing glance, and she was keen to engage in the conversation,

'Aw really, how is she? She must have finished Art College by now'.

Colm went on to say, 'She has mam, and she is working at the Deeside Museum'.

'Wow, that's the biggest museum in town, wow, good for her, I like Bernadette, as Jacqueline gave her son a hopeful look of, will you be seeing her again'.

'Before you ask mam, yes, I will be seeing Bernadette again mam, she looks amazing, and yes, we are going sketching together on Sunday, like we used to', said he

Jacqueline beamed with joy, 'That's wonderful son'.

Colm whistled away, as he walked up the stairs. Jacqueline felt a sense of romance that maybe on the way for her son. She would be happy with that.

Her thoughts turned to Niamh as it was a crucial year for Niamh at University, and she hoped she was not draining herself too much. I must call her in the morning to see how she is.

Emily arrived home just as Jacqueline had made her way to bed, they spoke briefly, Emily looked tired.

'I am having a night in tomorrow night mam, feeling a bit tired'.

'You are doing too much our Emily, let your assistants do more and you can concentrate on your wedding plans'.

'Yes mam, tomorrow I am just chilling and going through stuff for the wedding', said Emily.

Jacqueline informed Emily that she would be away for a few days and said,

'I am off to Glasgow staying overnight with my sisters'

Emily was excited for her mam, and didn't hold back in letting her know.

'Oh mam? that's fantastic, so glad you are getting out there'.

'You can look after things here, not that there is much to look after, your brother is quite capable of looking after himself', as Jacqueline winked at Emily.

They both laughed and hugged one another and said goodnight.

The night quickly drifted by, as Jacqueline awoke at 6am, she went over to the window and sat down at window seat. Her mind drifted back to her wedding day. It was a simple church wedding, and afternoon tea with the family. She couldn't get the image of Declan out of her mind at that moment, as he stood in the Church with the Navy-blue suit and very polished black brogues. She sighed and shrugged her shoulders.

'Enough! I must get myself sorted', as Jacqueline gave herself a little shrug to get a move one.

Sara and Aileen arrived at 7.00am, they would all get the train into Glasgow at 8.00am. Emily was hogging the bathroom as her mam shouted on numerous occasions,

Jacquline was getting impatient and shouted out,

'Come on now our Emily, you have had enough time in there don't you think, I have a train to catch!

Emily shouted back...

'I am finished! You should have gotten up earlier mam, especially when you have a train to catch'.

'Yes, I slept well for a change'. As Jacqueline gave her daughter a pensive look raising one of her eyebrows...

Emily looked at her mam with conviction,

'Good for you mam' and patted her on the shoulder as she made her way back to her room.

Colm surfaced out of his bedroom and said, 'No chance of me getting in the bathroom then'.

Jacqueline softly responded by saying,

'I won't be long son, just give me ten minutes.'

The household busied away getting themselves ready for their day. Emily left first as she was bracing herself for the open day of the new arts and crafts store adjacent to her Wool Shop, just two more days and it's launch day, she was so excited.

Colm was picking up Dylan as his car still wasn't fixed, Colm didn't mind he enjoyed his uncle's company into work.

Sara and Aileen had arrived, and Jacqueline was rushing around, so annoyed with herself for not getting up earlier.

'You ready yet our Jacqueline', as Aileen was getting a little impatient.

'Yes, let's go, doors locked, appliances unplugged, windows closed, yes, let's go'. As Jacqueline replied with a sigh ….

They were all dressed to impress, especially Sara, as she was tentatively thinking in her mind that John would be with a woman, and she wanted to look her best to make herself feel that bit better.

The train was on time, and they got themselves settled.

As Sara took her coat off, Aileen commented on her outfit, a rather fetching tweed jacket with a pencilled skirt and white blouse.

'Wow our Sara don't you look the impressionable girl about town'.

Sara's eyes widened as she said,

'Do you think so, I thought I would make an effort'.

'You certainly done that and more, your hair and make-up look fabulous girl'.

Jacqueline looked at Sara and whispered to her,

'You look amazing, John will be stunned'.

Sara smiled back at the sister and squeezed her hand. The journey was smooth, and they all sat back and enjoyed the scenery of some of the countryside.

They were almost in Glasgow as they gathered their belongings, it was a busy train, no doubt there were a lot of people travelling for the events in the business centre.

A quick taxi journey and they were all settled in at the Criton. Jacqueline suggested they had a cup of coffee in the restaurant area as they were still serving drinks to residents. Aileen was in total agreement on that score.

'What a good idea our Jacqueline, we can all catch our breath before making our way to the business centre'.

They sat for around fifteen minutes.

Jacqueline enquired how far the business centre was to walk, thankfully, it was a ten-minute walk through the high street, turn right through the shopping mall, and the business centre is based in the tall building on the right when you come off the mall.

Sara was surprised it was so close, 'We will be there in no time', as her stomach began to churn and churn. She was glad she hadn't eaten any breakfast as she was feeling a little nauseous.

They all walked briskly through the mall and into the business centre, it was packed with people. You had to sign in at the main reception, but they were not down on any of the lists, fortunately for them, there had been three cancellations, so they all got their badges to enter the seminars.

There were to be several seminars going on at the business centre and John was to be in the innovative seminar relating to new businesses, buying and selling. Sara was not sure why John was at the seminar? Her thoughts were that John had an ulterior motive for staying over in Glasgow.

Sara turned to Aileen, 'I had no idea that you had to sign in and book?' Aileen replied.

'I should have known that actually, Arthur has told me many times, just didn't enter my head, anyway, we are in, that is the main thing'.

The seating arrangements were not reserved so you could sit wherever you liked. As Sara made her way down the aisle first, John had spotted Sara and glanced over to her and her sisters, he looked shocked and surprised to see them at this event why?

John got up out of his seat and Jacqueline spotted him first with a young lady next to him, a brunette with her hair up in a bun, pretty she was, probably in her late 20s as Jacqueline observed her in detail.

John waved to Jacqueline and got out of his seat and made his way to them.

'Hello girls, what are you three doing here? As he looked at Sara with a surprising look on his face.

'You are looking stunning my love, confused as to why Sara was here? I wouldn't have thought this venue was your cup of tea'.

Aileen spoke first, 'I am here in place of my Arthur, he wanted me to see what was offer as he wants to expand the stationary business, he wanted me to make notes on all the ideas that may come up'?

John was a little concerned as to why Sara was here and looking so attractive, it stunned him completely.

Sara turned to her John with a confident look,

'Jacqueline and I are here my love to support Aileen, we all decided to go shopping afterwards and make a day of it, as you know Emily is getting married and we wanted to check out some wedding outfits; who is that you are sitting with?

Oh, as John looked a little sheepish, 'That is Rebecca, she is representative for one of sales companies that I buy from, I didn't know she was going to be here, we just bumped into one another'

Sara smiled back at John and said, 'We better take our seats the seminar is about to begin'.

As Sara took her seat, she looked like she was going to throw up, Aileen handed her a bottle of water. They sat for a while, and Jacqueline said, 'Let's not jump to conclusions hey', as she held Sara's hand.

The seminar was two hours long and everyone got out of their seats and made their way to the foyer, Jacqueline kept a close eye on John and Rebecca as they made their way to the bar area. They chatted for a while and Rebecca shook hands with John and left.

Sara looked distraught, Aileen squeezed her hand and said,

'I think Jacqueline is right, but we can still stay the night, you don't have to tell John we are staying over. Let's just question him on his next movements, is he staying over?

Jacqueline steered the girls to the bar area in John's direction. Aileen began to say,

'That was so interesting my Arthur will be pleased with what I have written in my notepad'.

Aileen began to quiz John,

'So, John, have you anymore seminars to attend, or was this the one, I notice this is a three-day event'.

John replied with a cautious look, 'I am down for two more which are tomorrow, I will let you girls go on your pre-wedding shopping spree'. He kissed Sara on the cheek with a poignant address,

'See you tomorrow night my love'.

Sara hesitantly answered, 'Tomorrow night what time, will you be late in'.

'I think so love, the last seminar is late on tomorrow, so yes, I believe so'.

Aileen knew then there was something not right as the last seminar was at 4.30pm and finished at 7.30pm so there was no way he should be late home...

Sara turned to her sisters as she screeched!

'I don't want to stay over; I just want to go home!

Jacqueline looked at Aileen and said, 'I think our Sara has had enough'.

'Yes, I think you are right'.

They all chatted for a few minutes and Sara pointed out that she would rather wait until John came home and had it out with him in private in their home. She felt she couldn't deal with it now, as she needed time to think things through. She thanked her sisters for being so supportive.

'Right, let's get on the train and get Sara home'.

Chapter 4

Jacqueline gave out a sigh of relief, she was home and glad to be. Just as she opened the door to be greeted by Colm, who spoke anxiously,

'Where have you been mam! Our Niamh has been calling you and calling you! She sounded anxious! She wouldn't tell me what was wrong mam?.

'Alright son, I will call her now'.

The telephone rang out for such a long time and Jacqueline began to get a little anxious, finally! Someone on the other end of the telephone.

'Hello, you reached Horsham Halls, who would you like to speak to'.

'Could you please fetch Niamh Gibson for me, it's her mam speaking'.

'Oh, her mam! Of Course, just a tick'

Niamh hurried from her room to the telephone,

'Mam, Jessica has been assaulted! Apparently, she is not the only one. We have been told to be very diligent and don't go out alone'.

Jacqueline was worried and her response was that of concern for her daughter's safety.

'Are you ok pet, do you want to come home?'

Niamh was adamant in her reply to her mam,

'No mam, not until the weekend, I want to stay here with Kate, Jessica is in a bad way, and she will be going home once she has been discharged from the hospital'.

'Well, if you are sure pet, but just you watch yourself at times mind'

Niamh felt a sense of comfort hearing her mam's voice as she began saying,

'You know me mam, I am as tough as boots, I must take after you mam. I just wanted to hear your voice to keep me grounded, I was scared for a while, you have made me less scared mam. It's so good to hear your voice.... again... I hope I didn't scare Colm I must have sounded a bit anxious, tell him his big sis is ok'.

'I will pet, just a few more days and you will be home, look after yourself pet, love you'.

'I will mam, love you too, see you Friday night, as Kate is going home on Friday night'.

'Alright pet, I am going to get Uncle Dylan to pick you up at 6pm'

'Ok mam, I will look out for him'.

Jacqueline put the telephone down and assured Colm that Niamh was alright, she was just a little homesick. She telephoned Dylan to pick Niamh up, as she knew he wouldn't mind once he knew of the circumstances.

Colm turned to his mam with a dutiful gesture,

'I will put the kettle on mam, you look like you could do with a cuppa'.

'Oh! Yes! Son that would be lovely'.

They both sat down at the table and Jacqueline calmly explained to Colm that he doesn't have to worry about his big sister, she is missing her home comforts, Jacqueline didn't want to divulge such a sensitive topic with Colm. It wasn't for her to discuss.

'Ok Son, I think you can just get yourself down to the fish shop tonight, we will have a takeaway lad, I am exhausted'.

'That sounds just to the ticket mam, your usual Cod and Chips'.

'Yes, let's just have lazy night, and watch the quiz show on TV tonight, that's if you are not going out with the lads.'

'Nah mam, I am having a night in with my mam'.

Jacqueline was surprised, but it was a lovely surprise, quality time with my son'.

Niamh at this time was getting ready for the meeting in the campus hall in relation to a spat of assaults that seemed to have occurred during the past few weeks.

The Police and Principal were hosting the meeting to give assurance to all the students. There were a lot of students making their way to the hall. DCI Steele had gathered his team to circulate the room and look for anyone who is showing signs of anything that looks out of the ordinary; for instance, if anyone is looking particularly nervous, or sweating for no reason? The young DC asked if that applied to everyone or just the male students in the room. DS Scott, smiled at the young DC and whispered to him,

'It's assault lad on young female students, so I would keep your eyes on the male students'.

The young DC looked embarrassed, 'I will do that, as he walked away across to the other side of the room'.

DCI Steele began the meeting and asked everyone in the room if they had any information in relation to the recent assaults, and they could come forward without reproach. Everyone would be treated with respect, and it is all confidential. He reiterated is appeal to all in the room.

The principal explained to everyone if they were struggling there will be a qualified counsellor on campus to assist anyone if needed and the details will be posted on the main board for anyone who wishes to sign up for that assistance.

The whole room was buzzing, everyone talking over one another, the sound began to get deafening as the principal urged everyone to take their seats and listen to the instructions from the DCI Steele.

'Listen up everyone, pay attention, we will be moving the chairs back and will be assembling four desks, so I want you all to form a line behind each desk in readiness for the interviewing process to begin. I do not want anyone to leave this building unless you told otherwise from me!'

Niamh and Kate stood back and engaged in a conversation which was all about Jessica, she had been brutally attacked, and they were so worried about her after her ordeal. She was with the Doctor and had been interviewed by with Police. She couldn't identify the culprit as he was wearing a masquerade mask, all Jessica knew was that he was well built and tall. He had this awful odour surrounding him. She said it smelt like some of kind perfume which was sickening.

The DCI approached Niamh and Kate and excused them as he had already spoken to them beforehand when they were comforting Jessica. He did point out to them both that if they recalled anything else to mind, they were to just call him straight away.

Niamh had given her statement to DCI

'I remember Jessica saying that he smelt disgusting, that awful smell, a perfume that had passed it sell by date'.

The DCI nodded back to Niamh and thanked her for that. Kate and Niamh linked one another as they left the hall.

Kate shuddered as they walked past the grassy edge where the attack took place it was all cornered off with police tape.

'I think I will go home now Niamh, it's almost teatime and it will be getting dark soon, I just want to get out of here, I am going to call my dad to pick me up'.

Niamh hugged her friend, and she made her way to the library, and she had almost finished her dissertation and just wanted to crack on with it and get it done. She had a few hours to go before her Uncle Dylan had to pick her up.

All the Policemen on duty were in the hall taking the statements and there was only one young police officer guarding the incident area.

It was starting to get dark, and Niamh was tentative of the time as she finished off her last paragraph and made her way through the library, it looked so empty, as she went through the reclining doors and down the curved steps.

The library was surrounded by trees and grassland; the pathway was long, and Niamh began to feel nervous for the first time since being at university. She could hear her own breath, and her breathing was getting faster and faster! She began to walk quickly with her haversack full of books. She thought she heard a rustling in the trees, but realised it was just the breeze or so she thought!

The masked man had seen Niamh go into the library and waited behind the bushes ready to pounce on her when she left the library. He came behind Niamh and pulled her to the ground! Tore into her blouse! She tried to scream! And gave out a faint yell! But there was no one around they were all in the hall!

As she struggled and struggled and tried to get hold of his mask, he slapped her hard and she was stunned! She pushed her books onto him, and he threw them across the grass and as he did so, Niamh lifted her right leg and kneed him so firmly into his groin and he screamed out so loud and fell! Niamh ran and ran! The young policeman pulled out his whistle and whistled for back up and ran into the bushes to where the attacker was, as the attacker was getting up, the young officer wrestled him to the ground and managed to put the handcuffs on him!

Niamh ran towards the hall; her face was full of blood and her clothes were all torn! DCI Steele grabbed hold of her and beckoned the Nurse to come forward as he made his way to the incident along with his fellow officers. The young officer at the scene had everything in hand, he had performed the arrest all on his own.

Dylan pulled up in the car park, and was astonished to see so many police cars, he began to feel at little uneasy as he made his way to the reception to collect Niamh. The Receptionist explained to Dylan what had happened, but he didn't really listen to all the conversation, he just ran for his life towards the hall to Niamh.

As he entered the hall, Niamh was with the Doctor and Nurse, he couldn't believe his eyes, he was stunned by her appearance, all he could say was, 'Our Niamh, not our Niamh!'

Niamh looked up at her uncle and said,

'Don't touch me, please don't touch me Uncle Dylan Please! As she cried out!

The Doctor took Dylan aside and told him that she will need to go to hospital, and she will need to be observed for the time being. She is going to need a lot of support.

Dylan had tears in his eyes at this point,

'She will have a lot of support, she has a loving family, I will call her mam to meet us at the hospital'.

The Doctor replied,

'You can call her here there is a telephone in the hall'.

Jacqueline answered the telephone and couldn't take anything in for a moment, but then she went into auto pilot and grabbed her coat and telephoned her sister Aileen to come quickly so she could drive her to the hospital. Aileen then called Sara to meet them at the hospital.

It was too much for Jacqueline at this point,

'My baby being attacked, it just not possible'.

She got into Aileen's car and began to get so angry and wanted answers how could this happen, how could they not protect the students, what is going on is what I would like to know. She was saying this in her own mind, not murmuring a word to anyone.

'How can I help my baby now; I must get it together and get in there and help her!'

Jacqueline ran into the hospital to be met by Dylan, he held Jacqueline and said,

'Just be prepared, don't crowd her and don't touch her as she doesn't want to be touched'.

Jacqueline looked distraught,

'Oh No! I won't touch her unless she wants me to '.

As they both moved towards Niamh's room the Doctor came out to speak to them and explained that he had given Niamh a sedative and she will be asleep for some time. The Doctor took them into a private room and explained to them that Niamh had been very brave, and the attacker did not penetrate her as Niamh managed to knee him in the groin and she ran. The Young officer on duty managed to apprehend the attacker.

Dylan held Jacqueline not knowing what to say as Jacquline broke down as she wept and wept. The Doctor left the room to give them some space.

Aileen and Sara entered the room, and they all sat together, Sara quickly went to get everyone a cup of tea. They sat for hours, Dylan suggested they come back in the morning, but Jacqueline was adamant she was not moving until she saw Niamh, she just wanted to see her daughter.

The nurse had popped in to bring them some blankets and promised to call Jacqueline if Niamh wakes up. It was 2am in the morning and the nurse appeared and shook Jacqueline to let her know Niamh was awake.

Jacqueline enter the room and Niamh cried out,

'Oh mam! you are here mam! as Niamh put her arms out to her mam.

Jacqueline held her and they cried together for a moment, as Jacqueline held her bruised face.

'Don't you worry about anything pet, your mam's here, you are going to be alright, you are!

Niamh was still sleepy with the strong sedative she had been given and fell asleep in her mam's arms.

Chapter 5

DCI Steele made his way to the interview room to the man who had attacked five women on campus over the past two months. It turns out that this young man's name was Adrian Snall, who had enrolled at Deeside University for the sole purpose of taking out these acts of violence. He was well known in Manchester as it turned out after DCI dug further into his past.

During the interview Adrian Snall appeared to be totally unremorseful, he was triumphant in his speech. He seemed oblivious to what the DCI was saying to him,

'You do realise you will be put away in prison for a long-time young man, do you not feel any kind of remorse for these young students.'

A loud sound of laughter resonated around the room from Adrian Snall, as he lay back in his chair and then moved forward. He spoke out with his aggressive tone,

'I love the power, and their determination to try and wriggle themselves free and especially when they scream out! He sat back again, with an arrogant smirk on his face.

The DCI almost swiped that grumpy smirk off his face. He played it by the book and constrained his anger as he left the room with the young DS. The DCI was livid, and his reproach was that of contempt,

'That young man is the most sadistic lad I have ever met in my whole career, we must through the book at him!

DCI Steele telephoned Jacqueline to give her the update on the case and assured her that Adrian Snall was going to prison for a lengthy period.

Jacqueline put the telephone down and sat in the kitchen staring at the clock for some time she was tentatively clock watching as Dylan was stopping by to pick her up, and they would head to the hospital to bring Niamh home.

'Two more hours, I must get her room all nice for her return, at least our Emily is still living here, that will be a great help to her', said she.

The doorbell rang, and Sara appeared. Jacqueline gave her sister and tight squeeze.

'Oh, sis lovely to see you so soon again, are you ok, you look a little pale again Sara, is everything alright with you, is it John, did you have the talk? Said Jacqueline,

'Yes, Jacqueline, we had the talk'.

'I best get the kettle on, and you can tell me all about it'.

Sara began to unleash the intense conversation she had with John.

We had such a flaming argument, and tempers were frayed, but the outcome was that John is was selling one of his businesses. One of the seminars was about that very thing. Hence why he was in Glasgow. It wasn't about another woman at all, it was about him surprising me with around the world cruise for my 35th birthday.

I am not sure if that is taking place now as the argument festered and we said things we didn't really mean, I think it's about trust now, and I feel I have let him down in some ways, but he had cheated that one time, I know it was such a long time ago, but he should not have been so secretive.

Jacqueline, held her sister's hand and said,

'He has to be aware that he has not been a saint, and surely, he can recognise that you still love him so much, let's face it, it's about the depth of your love and how you both can get passed this argument; it will be alright sis when he has calmed down, I am sure of that'.

Sara sighed and her eyes began to fill up with tears,

'I hope you are right our Jacqueline, I really do'.

'I am going to have to love you and leave you Sara, as Dylan won't be long as we are bringing Niamh home'.

'Oh of course! Sis, listen to me going on about me, when you have more important things to do'.

'Don't be silly Sara, it was nice to be diverted for a little time'.

They kissed and hugged each other, and Jacqueline hurried up the stairs to sort out Niamh's bed, she would put her favourite quilt on her bed; a patchwork quilt that Emily had made for her, and put her favourite book of poetry, John Keats on the bedside table.

Dylan pulled up outside the cottage he was early. Jacqueline opened the bedroom window and shouted to Dylan,

'The back door is open just let yourself in'.

Jacqueline quickly made up the bed and hurried downstairs.

'I just need to get my shoes, hat and coat on Dylan, I will be with you in a minute'.

Dylan replied,

'No rush Jacqueline, we have plenty of time'.

Jacqueline, asked after Serena and Dylan replied with a big smile on his face,

'She is blooming our Jacques'.

Jacqueline was so pleased for Dylan and Serena as she thought to herself,

'At least there is something to smile about it', as she sighed whilst putting her shoes on.

They both left the cottage and drove to the hospital, and Jacqueline wanted the happy conversation to continue as it was a lovely diversion to say the least.

Dylan was saying that Serena would love to have a girl, but if it wasn't the case, she be happy with either. He went on to say that Serena's mother was on a spending spree. She was spending a fortune on baby clothes, a cot and pram, it was in fact getting a little out of hand and Serena's father had to put his foot down to stop Charlotte from buying anymore for the baby.

Jacqueline was so surprised that Serena had let her run the show, as she knew Serena had her own firm ideas, it has not been easy for Serena to rein her mother in on this one, but she was so relieved that her father firmly put his foot down!

Dylan gave Jacqueline a wry smile,

'The wonders of bringing a baby into the world, it isn't as easy as we thought'.

Yes, Jacqueline replied, 'It is a game changer that is for sure'!

They had arrived at the hospital and Niamh was all ready to go, she looked very pale and didn't really want to talk very much; the journey home was very quiet. Jacqueline kept commenting on the sea view as Dylan thought it was a good idea to take the scenic route as it might be a calming journey for Niamh.

Niamh just stared out at the sea as the waves folded in and out.

Jacqueline spoke energetically,

'Aw look our Niamh there are the surfers coming out, it's a great day for them today, looks like the wind is good for surfing today'.

Niamh glanced towards the surfers with a vacant look, she was in a trance, and they didn't really register with her at all.

Jacqueline sat back and held her nervous stomach, she was thinking of ways in how to engage with Niamh and at this point she thought of Fr Donnelly and how he always came up with sound advice in a crisis.

'I will call him tomorrow, yes, I will call him', as Jacqueline muttered to herself.

Dylan parked the car and gave Niamh a big hug and whispered in her ear,

'Serena is longing to see you Niamh, when you are up for it, you just give me a call sweetheart.'

'I will Uncle Dylan, I will, next week perhaps'

Dylan was pleased that Niamh was thinking about it as he knew Niamh liked Serena a lot and they get on so well. He had decided to bring Serena around to see her the following week.

Jacqueline settled Niamh into her room and couldn't help but notice how Niamh seemed to be so happy to be home as she lay on the bed and picked up a collection of poems by John Keats

'You just rest now pet; I will make you a cup of hot cocoa with a chocolate biscuit'.

Niamh smiled back at her mam, and began reading the poem, 'Ode on Melancholy'.

'Make not your rosary of yew berries' as Niamh carried on reading the poem out loud to herself, she could feel Keats and his pain as if it were like her own pain.

She was elevated by the pure conviction of not letting yourself get into a sorry state but go out and embrace the beauty of nature. She felt comforted by this poem and delved more into its meaning, it was working, it was soothing her mind and her soul.

Jacqueline arrived with the cocoa and left Niamh to it, she smiled at her beautiful daughter and knew in her mind that the poetry would be a lovely distraction for her.

Niamh became so engrossed with the poems; she began to lose herself in the overall description of nature versus beauty. She was so engulfed in the poem, 'Endymion'.

'A think of beauty is a joy forever; its loveliness increases, it will never pass into nothingness'.

It's depiction of love as we know it, but it is overshadowed by the essence of pure nature,

'Such shapes of beauty move away the pall from our dark spirits; such the sun, the moon, tree old and young, sprouting a shady boon'.

Niamh felt a sense of calm and solitude that she hadn't had for some time, it was so soothing. Her eyes became heavy, and she fell into a deep sleep clutching the book of poems.

Jacqueline checked on her, and she smiled down at her daughter who looked so peaceful and left her undisturbed.

Emily came through the front door; she had been so busy with the shop and wedding plans. She stayed up for a while with Jacqueline to discuss the wedding arrangements. Emily was worried about her sister and wondered if she would be alright to go ahead with being a bridesmaid.

Jacqueline gave her daughter an assuring look,

'We have a few months yet to the wedding pet, don't worry too much, I know you have got a lot on your plate with the expansion of the wool shop, so just pace yourself and don't you overdo it', said she.

Emily smiled at her mam and responded,

'I will mam, Frankie is saying the same thing, you two are alike in many ways.'

'Good for him, it's great to have good son-in-law in the household', as Jacqueline smiled back at her daughter.

They both hugged each other and said their goodnights. Colm was already in bed, as he had a very early start in the morning. A rather big ship was coming into drydock, 'The Liston', it was coming in from the Atlantic and it was one massively big ship, lots to do for Colm, and Dylan for he was now the most senior engineer at the shipyard.

The night went by so swiftly and Colm was up at 5am, out the door at 6am, with his usual slice of toast in his mouth as he walked towards his car.

Jacqueline turned over in bed and took a quick glance at the clock,

'Oh, my goodness me! It's 7.00am already'.

She got out of bed and slipped her head around Niamh and Emily's bedroom. Niamh was sitting on Emily's bed; they were both crossed legged like they were still young teenagers. Jacqueline said surprisingly,

'Oh yes, what is this then, ladies of leisure I see, don't you know it's after 7am'.

Emily laughed aloud,

'Yes, well, I can be late today as Belinda is opening the shop this morning, so I am going to have quality time with my sis for a few hours', said she.

Jacqueline was so happy that Emily was doing that as she knew that Niamh needed her sister, as much as she needed her mam.

Emily asked her mam if she would do the honours and make some breakfast for them both, Jacqueline was happy do that.

Niamh was more than happy to keep the conversation going about the wedding and Emily didn't disappoint, as she didn't want to push Niamh on how she was really feeling.

The mood stayed light and happy, and they talked about how many bridesmaids would be in attendance and would there be a page boy. Emily was stuck with that one as she couldn't think of anyone. Niamh mentioned Kate's young brother so that was an option to think about.

Jacqueline arrived with two full plates of Bacon, Egg, Sausage and beans for the girls and Niamh made a good effort to eat some, as Emily was famished and ate the lot.

The morning went off so quickly and Emily went on her way to the wool shop. The extending property was looking so good with all its splendour. Belinda who was now lead assistant in the shop had designed the front window to perfection. She managed to mix and match the portraits made from beach stone, alongside the necklaces and earrings also made from beach stones. The Window display had a lovely banner above them, and it was named; 'The Pebbles on the Beach'.

Emily arrived outside and walked over the road to get a full view of the window display with all its vibrant colours. It complimented the Wool Shop next door with all its knitted colours and patchwork displays of teddy bears, dolls, and cushions. She was overcome with joy and praised the staff for their hard work they had been putting in these past weeks.

Niamh decided to take a walk along the beach towards the lighthouse as it had such great memories of when she was six years old, gathering all the seashells along the craggy paths, she was feeling poetic and just wanted to saunter slowly along the cracked pathways and rocky patches that lay on each side

She sat on the bench contemplating her life and it wouldn't be that long before she would get her results from the university, she wasn't sure now whether she would want to go into teaching given the trauma she still felt within her body.

Her thoughts strayed towards her dear friend Jessica, of whom she couldn't find the strength to call her, she felt guilty for avoiding her. Afterall, she was raped, and I was an attempted rape.

'Oh, how can I get past this God'.

She was surprised by her plea, as she wasn't that used with praying to God, she was a good catholic, but not as good as her mam, as she didn't go to church regularly. She thought maybe I should try, maybe I will find some peace maybe. She sat a while longer and made her way back home.

As she arrived home, she found Fr Donnelly in the kitchen and thought to herself,

'That was quick, I only just asked for help', as she muttered inwardly... She gave Fr Donnelly a warm smile and he reciprocated.

They sat for an hour and Niamh was soothed by his manner and his conversation of how to overcome despair and make it into something that is strong and full proof, it was rather like having a crutch to prop you up and it felt safe.

The day ended on a positive note for Niamh, a day of hope, but as she slept awhile the nightmares came upon her again and she relived the trauma, it wasn't going to be that easy, for what is easy ...

Chapter 6

It was a strange day in the Gibson house, as everyone was walking on eggshells so as not to upset Niamh, they were all trying too hard to engage with her and even the cheery notes of laughter seemed to be forced.

Niamh was building up to something as they all sat around the kitchen table on this Friday morning. Jacqueline was busy preparing breakfast and Emily and Colm were merrily chatting away about absolutely nothing that made much sense to Niamh. They were working hard on the conversation so as not to create any silent moments...

Niamh was at the end of her tether!

'Right, Everyone, please sit down! and listen to what I am about to say; I am getting a little drained with all the niceties and conversations that are inconsequential just so to avoid my assault! Yes, I was assaulted and yes, it is hard and yes, I am dealing with it, so don't, please don't tip toe around me like I am a precious doll to be taken care of, just please be yourselves. can you do that for me, please '

The room was as silent as a grave and Jacqueline was the first to speak.

'Ok pet we can all do that, yes, we have been tentatively trying to make things easier for you, and yes, it was not the right approach'.

Colm on a lighter note said, 'What does inconsequential mean?' Niamh laughed at her brother,

'Thank you, my dear bro, for such a ridiculous reply, because I know you know what that means, you were just trying to be funny'.

Colm cheekily winked at Niamh, and they all laughed together, that warmth of laughter resonated around the room, but Niamh hid her pain and embraced the warmth that was surrounding her, she missed it so.

Jacqueline began to open the conversation about Colm's meeting at the beach with Bernadette about their sketching expedition. He hadn't mentioned anything about it as he didn't want to appear so happy. In his mind, he felt that he was protecting Niamh in some ways as she looked so forlorn and unhappy.

Colm replied to his mam's question,

'Yeah, it was quite good we drew plenty of sketches together, we talked a lot about Bernadette's new job at the museum, she is loving it'.

Niamh smiled at her brother and said, 'Let's have a look at these sketches then shall we'.

Colm went up to his bedroom to retrieve his folder. Jacqueline and Emily left them to have a good catch up. Jacqueline was relieved to see a little sparkle in Niamh's eyes, as she loved Colm's sketches.

The sketches were mainly seagulls and birds, his favourite subject when sketching, although he did manage to do a rather good one of the rocks that were filtering around the sea- beds with their grassy stems protruding along the cliff top.

Niamh was so impressed with that one she asked Colm if she could have that as she wanted to get it frame. Colm didn't disappoint her, he was more than happy to part with it, which never happened with Colm he was rather protective of his drawings.

A knock came at the door, and it was Dylan and Serena coming to call, they were both worried about Niamh, and Serena had an idea that may interest Niamh.

As they all gathered in the living room, Jacqueline asked Serena how she was feeling, did she have any nausea? with her early stages of pregnancy. Serena was glowing and was so pleased she hadn't had any symptoms of nausea for some time. She was now 17 weeks pregnant.

Serena turned to Niamh and asked if she would like to accompany her to the stables to see Greengage her beloved horse.

'It is such a glorious day Niamh, and I know how you love the countryside; you can have a little turn around the paddock on little Maisy, as I know you are fond of her, what you think?'

Niamh was a little hesitant, but she did love Serena's energetic approach to life and yes, she hadn't seen Maisy in a good while.

They both hopped into Serena's car, as Dylan and Jacqueline looked on.

Dylan put his hand on Jacqueline's shoulder and said, 'How is Niamh, Jacqueline?'

Jacqueline with a concerned look replied,

'Oh, she is bearing up, being brave, but she is not coping underneath I am sure of that, perhaps she just needs more time, she won't see anyone about it'.

Colm entered the conversation with a confident manner,

'Our Niamh will get through this; I know she will'.

The conversation turned to Colm and Bernadette, he was not going to give anything away Colm, he was having the time of his life with Bernadette, but he wanted to keep it under wraps as he was convinced Bernadette was far too good for him.

In the meantime, Serena had pulled up at the stable and they made their way up to the paddock, Maisy was grazing she was getting bigger.

Niamh looked at her with a big smile on her face,

'Oh! Maisy you have gotten so big girl, what have you been doing since I last saw you'.

Maisy's eyes turned to Niamh, and she nodded her head up and down and made that joyful neighing sound. Niamh wrapped her arms around her neck. In that moment Niamh was so at peace with herself and she loved that feeling.

Serena brought Greengage out and saddled her up. Niamh turned to Serena and voiced her concern,

'You are not going to ride her Serena, are you sure you should in your condition'.

Serena smiled back and made her point clear,

'This may be my last chance to have ride around the paddock as I will be getting bigger soon, and I won't be able to mount her'.

Niamh walked Maisy around the paddock, as she wasn't a proficient rider, but one day she will be, she felt.

As Serena was about to mount Greengage a loud bang appeared from nowhere, it was a car's engine backfiring from the road opposite the paddock. Greengage bolted leaving Serena doubled up in pain on the grass.

Niamh sprinted towards her frantic! Serena cried out, 'My baby! My baby!'

There was a nearby telephone box on the open road, and Niamh tried to calm Serena.

'I will get help Serena, I will be two minutes, I need to get to that phone box, just hang on in there'.

As Niamh entered the phone box, there was a gentleman in the phone box, and she pleaded with him to hang up his call. It took him a few minutes to do so as Niamh eventually yelled out!

'There is a pregnant woman in the field, and she may die, so please get off the phone!'

The penny had dropped, and he moved away from the telephone. Niamh sprinted back to Serena she was crying out with pain and Niamh made her as comfortable as possible as they waited for the emergency services to come.

The sound of the sirens was bursting out! The ambulance was in sight, the relief on both of their faces as they held each other. At that moment Niamh had forgotten about her emotional pain as she was so consumed with Serena's pain; the transfer of emotions was so strong within her.

They eventually arrived at the hospital and Serena was immediately seen by the Doctors. Niamh hurried along to the telephone booth and called the house hoping that Dylan would still be there.

Dylan and Jacqueline were engrossed in the conversation of names for the newborn to be, Colm left them to it.

Jacqueline smiled at Dylan and said, 'Your brother would have been so proud of you Dylan, I am so happy for you'.

The telephone rang out and Jacqueline picked the receiver up.

'Mam! Oh Mam! it's Serena, she has had an accident, we are at the Annick Hospital!

'Accident what accident?'

Niamh replied, 'Greengage bolted as Serena tried to mount him, it was a car engine that backfired, it spooked him, and Serena fell to ground, she is so much pain Mam!

Jacqueline came off the phone and turned to Dylan and began telling him what had occurred.

The impression on Dylann's face was that of anger at first and then compassion, he couldn't understand why Serena would go riding, he was livid about that, but he was also upset about Serena being hurt. They both hurried to the hospital.

Entering the hospital Niamh greeted them and spoke with a tearful tone,

'They had taken Serena to surgery, they will let us know the outcome, we are to wait in the waiting room down the corridor'.

Distraught Dylan spoke, 'Surgery, oh my God, I hope she is ok and our baby!'

They sat in the waiting room for a few hours, and Dylan was getting rather impatient.

'I am going to find out what the hell is going on'.

As he got up to go the door, the Surgeon, Mr Compton appeared and asked them all to take a seat as began the prognosis.

'Serena has internal bleeding, with three cracked ribs. I am sorry to inform you, but we couldn't save the baby, we did everything we could. There is some good news, Serena will make a full recovery.

As they all looked at one another with shock and despair, Niamh began to cry incessantly. Dylan was inconsolable and left the room to take a swift walkabout outside. He needed the fresh air! He was raging with such mixed emotions as he muttered himself repeatedly.

'Why! why would she go riding, she had our baby inside, why would you do that'.

He took some time to gather himself and returned to the waiting room, Jacqueline and Niamh were not there, they had gone into Serena's room to see how she was.

Serena was still a little woozy from the anaesthetic, she cried out,

'Dylan! Dylan! Are you there?'

Serena opened her eyes, and everything was still a little blurry and she recognised Niamh and Jacqueline.

Oh, she said, 'My baby is ok isn't it, tell me that my baby is alright'.

Dylan entered the room and embraced Serena with a stern look on face,

'What were you thinking love to go riding in your condition, what possessed you'.

Serena began to cry as she spurted her words,

'My baby is alright though', with a pleading look at Dylan.

Dylan replied with tears in his eyes, 'I am sorry love, but you lost the baby'.

Jacqueline and Niamh left the room to give them some space.

The room was filled with tears and Dylan was wishing to withdraw from the room and quickly said.

'I will let you get some sleep love; the Doctor will be in soon'.

Serena looked at him with anguish, 'You are not leaving, you are not leaving me'.

'You need to rest love, and the Doctors need to see to you'.

Dylan couldn't wait to get out of the hospital, he was so full of resentfulness towards Serena at this time, he needed to get home and have a run along the beach to clear his head, he desperately needed that...

Jacqueline and Niamh walked towards Dylan, not knowing what to say to him.

Dylan rushed them into car and drove a little too fast, they were home within twenty minutes.

The goodbyes were so quick, and Niamh tried to console her favourite Uncle, but he wasn't having any of that, he began his angry mode, and Jacqueline knew how Dylan can get when he is in that kind of mood.

As Jacqueline closed the door, she put her arm around Niamh, and they made their way into the kitchen to make a cup of tea.

Niamh began to talk and talk about how she was feeling, and how her feelings had changed she was no longer in pain for herself but in pain for her uncle and Serena, their pain was greater than hers.

'I have to call Jessica's Mam tomorrow, I feel guilty that I have not been in touch, it was just too painful for me, but now I can face it'.

Jacqueline gave her daughter a caring look of pride,

'You are becoming the most extraordinary young woman my pet; I am so proud of you'.

They hugged for such a long time, and the door opened, and Colm entered the room with his dry sense of humour.

'Oh yes, what is this practising for dancing classes or what'.

They both let go of each other and hugged Colm.

Oh, he said, 'What I have done to deserve this then', as he winked at them both.

Niamh replied,

'Sit down our Colm, its Serena she has lost the baby'.

Colm looking stunned as he listened tentatively about what had happened, all he could think of was Dylan and how he will react.

The night was full of mixed feelings from all, and Jacqueline couldn't help but think of Serena and her parents. She was however more concerned about Dylan at this point as he was not taking this very well at all.

Sleep seemed to be the last thing on everyone's mind, it was getting late, and Emily had turned her key in the door, full of excitement about the new shelfing for the haberdashery side of the business.

The Wool Shop was holding its own next door, and she had plenty of staff now and she could now spend more time of the wedding plans. She was gushing with ideas and wanted to share them with everyone.

Jacqueline sat her down and told her of the day's events, she was gutted for her uncle and Serena, but she was so consumed with her life at that present moment, it took her awhile to let everything sink in.

Emily took to her bed and sat alongside Niamh and realised after a while that Niamh was starting to forget about herself, she felt that it may be a turning point for Niamh. She couldn't help but feel that this is good thing for our Niamh, as sad as it is, Serena can have another baby later, and our Niamh will get back to normal. She was hoping for a positive side to all of this.

Dylan could not see anything positive about this and finished his run, he had worn himself out, and began to drink his whiskey to blot out this awful day…

Chapter 7

Niamh awoke with a heavy feeling in her stomach, she was dreading the thought of speaking to Jessica, and re-living the awful assault, but she felt in her heart that Jessica's need was far greater than hers. She would wash and get dressed and telephone without hesitating.

The telephone rang out and eventually Jessica's mam answered.

'Hello Niamh, how lovely to hear from you, how are you doing?'

Niamh gave out a nervous cough and spluttered awhile before she could speak,

'I am doing ok Mrs Lowry, how is Jessica?'

Mrs Lowry was hoping Niamh would call on them soon, as she spoke earnestly,

'Jessica is seeing a Counsellor, she misses you and Kate, perhaps you two could come and visit soon'.

There was a quiet silence for a moment and Niamh replied.

'Yes, I will come to visit tomorrow, I will telephone Kate'.

Mrs Lowry sighed with relief, as she replied,

'Oh, that is good news Niamh, I will let Jessica know, shall we say lunch time and I can make a nice lunch for you all, how does that sound'.

Niamh agreed and as she said her goodbye, she sat at the telephone table with a great lump in her throat and gathered herself.

She picked up the receiver and telephoned Kate was happy to come along. Kate would pick Niamh up at 12.30pm.

Jacqueline came down the stairs and greeted Niamh.

'I heard voices were you on the telephone pet?'

Niamh explained to her mam what was happening, and Jacqueline couldn't be happier about this.

Jacqueline had been awake part of the night thinking through her own future. She was convinced that her journey into further education could be put on hold, as she didn't think it was the right time to devote herself to studying. Her Family came first.

'Come into the kitchen Niamh, I want to talk to you', said she.

Niamh looked at her mam inquisitively,

'This sounds ominous', as she smiled at her mam.

They sat down and Jacqueline began to say that she was going to put her studies on hold as it was only eight weeks away for enrolment and it wasn't the right time.

Niamh was cross with her mam, as she got up and spoke.

'Mam! this is not happening, you are not giving up your studies because of what has happened to me, I will not have it, Mam! I won't! This will make me feel worse, so please don't do this!

Jacqueline was shocked and surprised by Niamh's reaction, she was in fact stunned by it!

They both embraced one another, and Jacqueline put her hands on Niamh's face,

'I have underestimated your strength, and conviction, I had forgotten you are so much like me'.

They both shed a tear, and Emily was making her way downstairs, and was a little concerned about what she was witnessing in front her as she spoke out.

'Hey, you two what is this, can I join in too'.

Niamh moved towards Emily and said,

Everything is fine our Emmie; I have sorted mam out she was going to put her studies on hold'.

Emily smiled at them both and put her views forward on the subject,

'Well Mam, you know what our Niamh's like when she has a bee in her bonnet'.

Jacqueline smirked,

'I do indeed'.

Colm was singing in the bathroom, and they all looked at one another, and said out loud together,

'He has the love bug', as they laughed out loudly.

The laughter didn't last very long as the telephone rang out, Jacqueline answered it, it was Serena's mam on the telephone.

'Hello Jacqueline, have you seen Dylan he has not been to hospital since yesterday morning, Serena is so distraught as you can imagine, I have called him several times, but he does not answer'.

Jacqueline was now getting concerned and said she would call on Dylan and let her know.

Colm was standing at the top of the stairs and overheard the conversation and shouted down to his mam,

'I will drive mam; I will be five minutes.'

As Colm pulled up at Dylan's house, his car wasn't there?

They knocked just in case, but no answer, Colm turned to his mam.

'I will drop you back home mam, Dylan may have gone into work as they have a new Ship in Drydock this morning'.

Jacqueline was confused,

'Why hasn't he called at the hospital?

That warm feeling of happiness and expectation of it wanting to last longer had left Jacqueline's mind in an instant her thoughts were fixed on Dylan and Serena as she entered the cottage with a subdued look on her face.

Colm had arrived at work, and he telephoned the engine room, and was told Dylan was down below on the ship, 'Wilston'. He made is way down the gang plank towards the engine room and eventually caught up with Dylan.

Dylan looked up from the portside, and spotted Colm.

'Hey lad, what you are doing down here?'

Colm gave his uncle a concerned look and didn't hold back,

'Serena's mam has been trying to get hold of you, why are you not at the hospital, you should be there Uncle Dylan?'

Dylan got up rather sharply and steered Colm into a private space and looked sternly at him and raised his voice!

'Look, this is none of your business, and I have a job to do as you can see and that is what I am doing, I suggest you go and do your job in the drawing office where you belong'.

Colm took a step back and put his hands up and replied with a similar stern look of disapproval.

'Ok Uncle Dylan if that is the way you feel about it, then yes, I will leave you to it'.

As Colm walked up the gang plank, he was worried, he had never seen his uncle like this before, he was also worried that he could still smell alcohol on his breath as they were locked in the conversation.

He arrived back at the office and telephoned his mam to let her know he was at work, and he wanted to get on with the job in hand. He kept his own thoughts to himself...

Jacqueline at this time, was ruminating as walked up and down the kitchen, before she decided to make herself a cup of tea. As she sat, she murmured to herself,

'Oh, come on Jacqueline, you need to make a telephone call to Serena'... it wasn't going to be an easy conversation.

The conversation got heated on Charlotte's side of the call, and she let Jacqueline know that Serena was going to be discharged in a few days, and she would be coming home to their house to recuperate.

As Jacqueline put the telephone down, she kept thinking of what Declan would do? she started talking to herself.

'Why are you not here Declan when I need you!'

The day was becoming rather irritating now as Jacqueline decided to take a walk along the beach as the clouds had lifted and there was a lovely glimmer of sunshine, as she smiled up at the sky. A long brisk walk along the seashore was just what she needed.

Her favourite tree was just over the hill passed the craggy path that overlooked the shimmering sand that glared up at Jacqueline. She brushed her shoes into sand, not caring that her shoes would fill with the sand. she just wanted to feel the sand flowing over into her shoes for some reason. As the sand seeped into her feet she sat on the craggy rock and took her shoes off and dusted herself off.

The oak tree yonder swaggered in the breeze and Jacqueline admired its tenacity. She got to her feet and walked further down the beach. The appearance of a divine figure was approaching. They're stood Fr Donnelly, as he waved his biretta towards her. He was a welcomed interruption, Jacqueline was so pleased to see him, as she was just thinking about paying him a visit.

They both sat on the craggy rock and Jacqueline began to unfold the events that had recently occurred. Fr Donnelly listened patiently and responded with a thoughtful solution.

'I will pay Serena a visit today before she sets off home, I am sure all will be well when the dust settles, they are too much in love to abandon such a gift'.

Jacqueline replied and said, 'It is Dylan I am concerned about he has not been to the hospital and has become distant with us all'.

Fr Donnelly looked a little concerned and said to Jacqueline that he would also pay Dylan a visit. Jacqueline was not keen on that solution, as Dylan was not in a good place. Father Donnelly was insistent that he would call on Dylan, as it didn't matter to him if Dylan was rather cool with him. He had known Dylan all his life and he knew he could be rather standoffish and prickly. It was his welfare that Fr Donnelly was concerned about.

They both sat and took in the cool breeze as Fr Donnelly made a comment about the calmness of the sea.

'It always amazes me nature and the calmness of the sea, it can be brutal, and it can be kind, just as life is, we embrace the same and look to the future, and grab by its neck, it's pain and its joy, it is hard to make sense of it, but we work it out eventually'.

Jacqueline smiled at Fr Donnelly, and thanked him for his support, as they both walked up the hill to her cottage. He bid Jacqueline goodbye and made his way to his car parked along the coast road. Jacqueline felt at ease for a moment and hoped all would go well with Dylan and Serena.

Serena was so upset that Dylan had not been to see her, she started to resent him more and more as the days went on. Her mam and dad were at her side, and they were not impressed at all with Dylan. Her father was extremely disappointed in Dylan, as he was just starting to really like him a lot. He turned to his daughter and spoke with his persuading argument,

'You come home for a little while at least until you are feeling stronger love, I think that is the best thing to do just now'.

Serena, nodded with a tear in eye,

'I would like that dad, I don't want to see Dylan, I really don't'.

Charlotte was really worried about Serena as she knew she didn't really mean that it was just the loss and pain she was suffering right now.

Fr Donnelly knocked politely on the door adjacent to Serena's bedside, and she sat up directly looking rather surprised to see him, as she looked up and said,

'Hello',

'He warmly reciprocated with an uplifting tone in his voice',

'Now how are we getting on here, I hope they are treating you well, I am sure they are, you will be wanting to get home soon I bet, nothing like your own bed to sleep in'.

Serena was taken back by his jovial manner, as he didn't come out with the usual condolences, which she found rather refreshing at that moment, it was if she was back to normal, for a moment anyway.

Serena's parents left the room and let Father Donnelly and Serena have a private chat, as they felt it might give her some peace of mind at least.

Father Donnelly sat awhile patiently just waiting for Serena to release her thoughts and feelings, it wasn't too long before she gushed and gushed with the pain and her resentfulness she felt for Dylan. He just sat back and let Serena get it all out and then he began to say to her,

'It may not sound right to you, but it is good to feel the pain, because you can learn to live and get over it in time, I know it's not a wonderful thing, but life is hard at times and we live with our emotions and they get tested to the limit sometimes, but don't forget what a wonderful caring person you are and you will get over this. I believe you and Dylan will sort things out in time, give yourself that a bit of space for now'.

Serena put her hand on Fr Donnelly's cuff, and as she looked up at him, he spoken in such a soothing way, it seemed to calm her somewhat.

'I cannot thank you enough for coming, you have given me some sort of strength, I don't know what, but it feels strong, so I will take time out and try and heal at home at my parents for a little while, I think its best'?

Father Donnelly, responded by saying,

'Don't leave it too long to go back home, I think you will know when it is time to go home'.

Serena felt exhausted after Fr Donnelly left her with those thoughts, and she was left alone as she lay down on her pillar and a certain ease came over her, like a soft breeze brushing her face, she fell into a deep sleep....

Father Donnelly drove to Dylan's apartment, but there was no reply, as he sat in his car and looked at his watch,

'Well, its 6pm, maybe he has been caught up at work?'

He decided to make his way back to Presbytery and telephone the shipyard. The receptionist answered the telephone with a bright and breezy voice,

'Good afternoon, Walls Drydock, Helena speaking how can I help you'.

He was taken back by such a spritely tone of voice; he asked if he could speak to Dylan. The receptionist informed him that there was some problem in the engine room and Dylan was in attendance. She wasn't aware at this time there had been an accident, and three men were badly burned...

Chapter 8

The port side of the ship,'Wilston', was becoming a major problem as one of the valves in the engine room had leaked badly causing a small explosion and the steam rose heavily and caught three of the men nearby who were badly burned. Dylan was at this time trying to fix the valve to avoid any further explosion.

He managed to reach the cupboard as he fumbled around for the heat-resistant gloves, they fell on the floor next to him. The flames began to spark, and it was getting serious now. The alarm button was not close by, and Dylan crawled along the floor until he got close. He got on his knees and pushed himself up with great force to ring the alarm bell. He fell back down and put his mask back over his face. The rest of the crew were reaching for fire extinguishers, unfortunately, one of them wasn't working. They all tried in vain to dimmish the flames which were spreading, and the smoke was rising.

Dylan was getting frantic trying to get everyone out as he was feeling a little ashamed of himself, he had drunk one too many whiskeys the night before. He was now feeling fully alive and alert, and he made sure the men were out. He dragged himself across the floor and made his way to the hatch, it was stuck, he lay there feeling the effects of the smoke, and he could feel himself becoming less and less conscious, all he could think of was Serena, he then passed out.

The Fireman arrived and took the hatch door off and dragged Dylan to safety, the paramedics were on board and quickly set to their task to revive Dylan. It wasn't too long before Dylan was stable, and he was driven to Teesside hospital.

Colm was on the deck and followed Dylan to the hospital, he would telephone Jacqueline as soon as he arrived at the hospital. Dylan was murmuring away about the men,

'How are the lads, are they alright'.

Colm calmed him and said, 'Yes, Uncle, they are doing ok, you rest now'.

The other three engineers, Stan, Simon, and Billy had suffered severe burns on the legs and back, but they were going to be ok. The Surgeon had informed their families that once stable they would be able to have skin grafts in a few weeks' time.

In the meantime, Colm had telephoned Jacqueline to let her know the outcome. Jacqueline stood silently for a moment and said,

'I cannot believe this, as if he hasn't had enough pain lately, I must telephone Charlotte so she can let her daughter Serena know what has occurred.

Colm said that he would be staying with Dylan for a while. Jacqueline replied by saying,

'I will call Serena son; you stay where you are'.

Jacqueline put the receiver down and telephoned Charlotte to let her know what has happened to Dylan.

The telephone rang out and rang out and just as she was about to put the receiver down, Serena's father answered the telephone.

Jacqueline stammered for a moment and said,

'Hello Mr Inskip, it's Jacqueline speaking, I wonder if I could speak to Charlotte'.

He replied rather coldly, 'What is it about, why can't you speak to me'.

Jacqueline stunned by the response, answered back in a rather cool tone,

'Well, actually it is Dylan he has been in an accident at work, and he has suffered superficial burns, I thought it only right to call you and let Serena know what has happened to her husband'?

Mr Inskip replied by saying,

'Serena is in no state to receive or comprehend any more trauma currently, I think it is best to just keep this under wraps for now, I am sorry that this has occurred, I am sorry he has been hurt, but we are all hurting at the loss of the baby.

Jacqueline was amazed at Mr Inskip's response it was as if they were strangers, she couldn't comprehend such a response, she gave herself a minute and responded with such vigour,

'Now look here Mr Inskip, Dylan and Serena are married! Husband and wife and she has the right to know what has happened to her husband, I must insist on speaking to her directly if you do not mind'?

As Mr Inskip was just about to reply abruptly to that response, Serena had entered the hallway and asked her father who it was on the telephone, he turned to his daughter and said,

'It is Jacqueline, don't you get upset'.

Serena looked confused as she called to her father,

'What do you mean, what has happened dad, here, give me the telephone, I will speak to Jacqueline myself'?

Jacqueline began telling Serena what had happened she quickly put the telephone down and gave her father a rather angry look and lashed out at him.

'Dad, you had no right keeping this from me, you can make amends and drive me to the hospital right away, no arguments, I would drive myself but as you know I am not allowed for a few weeks, so can we please go now'.

Mr Inskip reluctantly picked up his car keys and escorted Serena into the car. Charlotte followed on as she knew she may have to keep the peace. She had sat in the backseat refereeing if needed...

The journey was frosty to say the least, but they survived it, and Serena quickly made her way to Dylan, who at this time was placed in the emergency bay until they could find him a bed.

He was sedated and Serena was told to wait until the Doctor had seen to him, they would call her when she could go in and see him.

Mr Roberts, the surgeon came to the waiting room to let Serena know she could go in and see him.

'He is rather groggy at the moment, so don't expect too much, he has superficial burns to his right arm, so don't be alarmed at the sight of his arm'.

Serena was so overwhelmed as she bent over to Dylan, she loved him so, and the pain she felt of losing her baby, had transferred to Dylan; she knew he would be in such pain when the painkillers wore off, all she could think of was she was so glad that he was alive as it could have been worse.

She held his hand for such a long time and listened to his moans and groans, as he shouted out to his men to shut the valves off!

She lay in the easy chair for some hours and quietly fell asleep. The door opened and in walked Colm with an anguished look on his face, as he stood over Dylan's bed. He couldn't help thinking about their last conversation which wasn't pleasant, and Colm had never had such a fall out with his uncle, he was concerned about his well-being.

Serena slowly awoke from her light sleep, rubbing her eyes, as she looked up and caught a glimpse of Colm sitting by Dylan's bed. She spoke first,

'Hi Colm, it is good to see you, how are you, it has been a while since we last saw you'.

Colm looked towards Serena and replied,

'Yes, it has been a while since we last spoke, are you ok Serena, I know it has been such a hard time for you too, Dylan hasn't been himself since you, you know', as he awkwardly tried to avoid bringing up her miscarriage.

Serena, looked pale and drawn, and went over to Colm and put her hand on his shoulder and said,

'I know, it has been hard for the both of us, I feel so guilty Colm', as she began to cry.

Colm put his arm around Serena to console her with such reassurance,

'You must not blame yourself, accidents happen, and you two will be ok, just give yourself time'.

Serena couldn't help but notice how grown-up Colm had become he was older for his years, not yet twenty years of age.

They sat for some time, Dylan was in and out of consciousness, and the Doctor had arrived so they both went to the restaurant to have a sit down and a coffee, as they made their way down the corridor, Serena's mum was walking towards them.

Colm made himself scarce as he felt they needed time together. He made his way back home to update his mam on the situation. He was tentative of the time, as he was on his break from the office and needed to get back.

As Colm arrived at the office, he was informed that an investigation had taken place, and it was concluded that there were two faulty valves in the engine room, and it was not down to human error. Colm was so relieved as he sat back in his chair, as he knew that Dylan would blame himself. He would return to the hospital later that day to give Dylan the good news.

As he pulled up at the car park outside the hospital on a bleak Wednesday evening the heavens had opened, he quickly put on his anorak and sprinted into the hospital entrance,

'Oh, should have parked closer'., as he muttered to himself.

Serena and Charlotte were by his bedside and Dylan was wide awake, he was holding on to Serena's hand. Dylan had a worried look on his face as Colm approached his bed side.

Colm smiled at Dylan and said,

'I have got some good news for you Uncle, some very good news'.

Dylan replied with a sigh,

'Oh, what is that then'.

Colm winked and replied,

'The investigation into the accident in the engine room concluded earlier today by passing a verdict of faulty valves, there was no human error'.

Dylan sat up rather quickly and said,

'I knew it, I knew it, that valve near the portside was giving me trouble from the start; how are the other lads doing?'

Colm looked away for a moment and eventually let Dylan know the extent of their burns.

Dylan was mortified, as they were nearest the portside and caught the brunt of the explosion. He was glad they would be making a full recovery. He lay back on his pillow and Serena could see he was in pain and asked the nurse to step in.

Charlotte and Colm left the room and sat outside. There was an awkward silence as Colm didn't really know Charlotte that well, only to say hello. He recalled meeting her at Serena and Dylan's engagement party, and there was mention that Charlotte had painted in her earlier days, but she gave it up when Serena was young, he never knew why though. He wanted to bring the subject up as he was familiar with painting and drawing, but he didn't want to put his foot in it. It was Charlotte who spoke first.

'How do you like working as a draughtsman at the shipyard, I know you sketch a lot'.

Colm looked surprised Charlotte knew so much about him, and answered,

'I love working as a draughtsman, I still sketch at the beach at the weekends, do you like sketching?'

Charlotte went silent for a moment and then began to speak,

'I do, actually, I have not done a lot of sketching for a long time, but I do plan to sketch again, in fact I was just talking about it to your mother the other week, I am building myself up to do a full sketch, I am taking baby steps at the moment'.

His response confidently shone through, and Charlotte was getting rather excited at the prospect of sketching again...

'Oh, you must, you must, there is nothing like drawing it such a joy and it is a great relaxer, I feel you can just get lost in your picture and how it develops, so satisfying'.

She invited him to come and visit them that weekend, to view some of Charlotte paintings. Colm was more than happy to oblige; he was quite excited about it.

They had both got lost in their conversation and Charlotte had not noticed that her husband had arrived, he was getting rather anxious as he had not received a call from her with an update. Colm got up out of his chair and said his good-byes.

Mr Inskip had a rather confused look on his face as he turned to Charlotte,

'What was that about? See you on Saturday?'

Charlotte smiled at her husband and said,

'Colm is a great sketcher, and I have invited him to come along to our house on Saturday to view my paintings that are stuck in the basement, I must sort that out before Saturday'.

Mr Inskip couldn't be happier as he felt that his wife had buried her life of paintings forever, he was so delighted that Charlotte opening herself up to painting again, and he noticed that her face was glowing with excitement. He wanted to thank Colm in person when he calls on Saturday.

In the meantime, Serena and Dylan were having their heart to heart, as they poured their heart and soul out to each other, their love was so deep and strong, the pain and loss they were feeling was now bound together. Serena lay on the bed next to Dylan as they both fell into a quiet sleep....

Chapter 9

The following day Niamh was getting ready to head to the University for the first time since her assault as she was determined to be there as it was results day!

Jacqueline was also poised for her eventful day as she was heading to the college to sign up for her first course in Higher Education, she was torn between the aspect of English or Creative Writing.

Niamh wished her mam luck with her day and they both sat for a moment in the garden to feel the fresh air on their faces. It was frosty day, and the breeze was a welcome quest in their eyes because they both loved a good old frosty morning to get those brain cells going...

As they discussed their plans, Niamh turned to her mam and said,

'I will drive you to the college mam, I know I am not due at the University for some time, but it is no bother mam'.

Jacqueline, looked up at her daughter with a caring smile, and said,

'That's ok pet, Aileen is dropping by, and she will take me, as we are going shopping afterwards.'

Niamh was relieved in a way, as she needed time to reflect, and she was going to call around to see Jessica before she headed to the University.

Aileen had arrived to pick Jacqueline up. The sun was shining so brightly now, and she suggested that go along the coast road; the scenic route ten minutes out of their way to the college, but it was always a refreshing journey.

Jacqueline wound the car window down to feel that sultry breeze once again. It melted on her forehead, she was feeling relaxed and consumed with the view, the sea view, and its splendour. She was feeling very poetic, and felt a verse come into her head.

    A sea of dreams, those glorious seams of threaded delight...

That muster into a sequence so light, so light….

Jacqueline held her head back and breathed in the salty air, and she decided at that moment that she would sign for both courses, she had the time. A satisfying pause made her feel so light and confident with it.

They had arrived and Jacqueline walked with a spring in her step and was so happy to have concluded her final decision of both subjects.

Aileen was so proud of her sister, they both had a change of plan in relation to shopping as the day was so full of sunshine and goodness, it had to be a beach, lunch at the sea-bowl bistro. The shopping could be done another day.

As they arrived at the sea front, Jacqueline took a moment to think about her Niamh, and hoped it would go well, she felt in her heart that it would.

Niamh telephoned Jessica and they both went to university together. She was over the moon and told Jessica she would pick her up. Kate would be there, so the trio was complete. The threesome was back together again, they had been through a lot at the University, especially Jessica and Niamh…. It seemed to make them stronger in each other's company, they fed off their determination to try put the dreadful assaults behind them.

As they all met up in the Hall at the University to collect their results.

The three of them headed to their favourite spot by the lake, Jessica asked Niamh to open her envelope.

Niamh jumped up and down and said loudly,

'Jessica, you are going to be a designer! you have gone and got a 2:1 degree', Jessica was able to complete her Art/English Degree.

Niamh held her dear friend Jessica as she wept with joy.

Kate sat with her envelope and pondered as she was the one who wanted her history degree so badly, she wanted to be able to advance as a curator or historian in the local museums, she was hoping for a 2:1 to get her there.

She slowly opened the envelope and passed it to Niamh, Niamh sprung into a high leap and turned to Kate and said,

'Oh, our Kate! You have excelled yourself girl, you have a first-class degree!'

Tears and joy, sprung from every corner and Kate shouted,

'It's your turn now Niamh, as Niamh passed her envelope to Jessica, and slowly composed herself for Niamh was desperate to get to teaching college to become a teacher'.

Jessica opened the envelope and wept and wept, Niamh wasn't sure whether they were tears of joy, or of despair; a moment lapsed, and Jessica put her arms around Niamh and passed the envelope to her to read; First Class degree in English.

Niamh was numb, stunned, amazed, she couldn't believe such a thing had occurred she was sure it would be a second-class degree. They all huddled together in that moment and decided they would have a night out and celebrate. Before that happened, they all rushed to the telephone booths to call their parents.

Niamh was unfortunate not to connect with her mam, as she remembered her mam would be out shopping with her Aunt Aileen, or so she thought.

They all said their good-byes and would meet at the Sea-bowl bistro at 7pm.

As Niamh pulled up at the cottage, she was too excited to be indoors, she put her plimsoles on and walked along the beach, towards the lighthouse, as she passed by the Sea-bowl bistro, she heard someone shouting, 'Niamh!'

She looked over and could see her mam coming towards her, Niamh couldn't control herself and wept with joy, as her mam held her.

'I did it mam, I did it, I got a first, a first-class degree, can you believe that mam'.

Jacqueline wept alongside her daughter and said,

'I am not surprised, 'bright spark', you have always been a bright spark, who lights up my day and every day after'

Aileen congratulated her niece, and they all went inside to have lunch, Aileen was adamant that Niamh should have a celebratory drink, Niamh replied with,

'Just a small one, as I am heading here tonight with the girls, and we are then going on to the 'Lantern' afterwards. We have all done well, so well'.

Aileen brought Niamh a small glass of red wine to celebrate. They all decided to walk their lunch off along the beach and dipped their feet in the sea for good luck, not that any of them needed good luck it was a feast of a day, it really was.

As Jacqueline and Niamh arrived back at the cottage it was almost teatime and Emily and Colm would be home soon, Jacqueline prepared a quiche potato salad for Colm and Emily's arrival home.

Emily was first home and so proud of her dear sister Niamh, as they sat together. Colm came in through the back door and shouted,

'What's all this excitement I hear in this house as Niamh and Emily were animated and talking and giggling out loud'.

Colm was elated for Niamh as he shouted out!

'Brain box, I knew you would do it our Niamh'.

The conversation flowed and flowed until tea was over, as Emily had some exciting news of her own, as started to let everyone know that the wedding outfits were ready for the first fitting on Saturday. She turned to her brother Colm and said,

'Bro you are going to the tailors with Frankie and his dad to get suited and booted', as she winked at her brother.

Colm winked back and said, 'No bother sis, I will be there'.

Jacqueline turned to her daughter as she whimsically pointed out to Emily,

'I see you have been busy, lass, busy indeed', as she smiled warmly at her dear daughter.

Emily put her arm around her mam and couldn't help but to give a whimsical reply,

'You as well mam, you are booked for your outfit next door to the bridal shop. I have covered everything, after all, mam, its 6 weeks away, which is not that far away. I needed to get a wiggle on as the shop displays and promotions are all happening in the next month'.

Jacqueline gasped in awe of her daughter who seemed to be multi-tasking to the hilt! This management role had certainly brought the best out of Emily. She couldn't be prouder of her three children, if only Declan could have been here, as she turned away and gave herself a secret sigh, as her heart sank, but she was not going to let it show in any shape or form, it was going to be a joyful evening.

Niamh made her way upstairs to get ready for her night out, Emily followed behind her and as they both entered bedroom and sat on the bed.

'Well, our Niamh what are you wearing tonight to celebrate,' said Emily.

Niamh didn't really know as she hadn't been on a night out since the attack at the University. Suddenly, she seemed to have come down to earth in that moment and felt a little shudder at the thought of going out again. Emily was aware of this as she could feel her sister's despair, it was that look she gave her, Emily knew that look.

They sat a while longer and Emily responded quickly by saying.

'I know what you going to wear, this is a celebration; my sister, the brain box of the family, is going out in style, no reservations, no apprehension, no fear, that is an order'.

Niamh smiled at Emily and couldn't believe her enthusiastic sister, who is braver than any of us, she overcame her asthma and fear when she was younger and steered bravely into doing what she does best, creating something out of nothing.

As Emily got all the outfits out of the wardrobe and onto the bed she began to mix and match and eventually they agreed on the pastoral silk leafed blouse. Niamh loved her wide legged navy trousers, and her navy small stiletto heeled sling backs. The pastoral blue head band completed the outfit.

'The headband gives you attitude, and it shows off your lovely hair and your gorgeous face girl' said Emily,

Niamh laugh out loud,

'Well, I don't need a fan club, I have got one here', as she laughed so loud,

Colm entered the conversation by saying,

'Wow, this is some party right here by the looks of it as he jumped on the bed'.

Emily slapped his leg with a cheeky reply.

'You watch the clothes bro, just move that backside of yours' Colm grinned back at them,

'I think that's my exit', as he gave them a wry smile.

Emily asked how she was getting to the Bistro, Niamh said she would get a taxi.

Colm butted in with his kind request.

'I will take you sis, I am not doing anything tonight, no bother sis'.

Niamh hugged her brother with a loving response,

'You are a star bro, love you'.

Colm's head swaggered side to side as he replied.

'There is no need to go that far, I will be downstairs, as he laughed out loud.

Niamh began dressing and Emily left her to it.

It was 6.30pm the sun had gone down and as Niamh looked out of the window she shivered for a moment and was so glad Colm was giving her a lift, as she felt at little uneasy at the prospect of having a night out, it had been such a long time since she last ventured out at night…

Colm gave Niamh a shout, she was ready, as came downstairs her Mam and Emily put their arms around her and spoke simultaneously,

'Go have a great night out pet, you deserve it'.

Colm whistled down the path as he opened the car door for Niamh, saying,

'Your carriage awaits princess'.

Niamh knocked his arm and gave him a sarcastic response,

'You just love winding me up, don't you'.

Colm couldn't resist, he wanted Niamh to feel relaxed and to have a good night.

As they drove to the Bistro Niamh turned to Colm and asked him about Bernadette and how things were going with him.

Colm was reluctant to engage in the subject, he didn't like talking about his love-life as he was enjoying too much, and felt if he expressed too much, it might put a damper on the relationship; he was a little superstitious in that way. He didn't really know why that was, but he wanted the relationship with Bernadette to flourish, and felt it wasn't quite the right time to say it out loud, so instead he answered his sister with a casual reply

'Bernadette is fine, we are just good friends, we get on ok'.

Niamh changed the subject to his work, of which Colm was so relieved about, he spoke energetically about his week and the new arrival of the ship, 'The Amber'. Niamh was excited for her brother, and they talked awhile as he pulled up outside the Bistro, they were early.

They sat and carried on their conversation, which included Dylan, and Niamh was relieved to hear about Dylan and Serena reconciling their differences.

As Colm looked up, he spotted Jessica and Kate coming towards them, and Niamh got out of the car and gave her brother a kiss, he was taken back by it, as it had been a while since his sister had kissed him on the cheek, he was happy to receive it.

They all went inside and ordered their celebratory drinks; it was going to be one bottle of white wine and one bottle of red wine. They all made their way to the decking at the rear of the bistro, it was a lovely night, and it wasn't that cold for a change. The bistro was lit up with lanterns and small little sequence of lights that were below the decking, you could see the shadow of them from the corner of eye.

There was a band playing at nine thirty, it was a trio, 'The Triplet's; a young man playing the piano, and older man in his 50s playing the violin, and there was one female singer, which complimented the male players of the trio.

They were all relaxed and chatted away until Jessica noticed a group of lads who were looking over to them for such a long time. There was one who was almost six-foot tall, brown hair, hazel eyes, he looked like he was fixated on Niamh.

As they began to talk about this group of lads, Niamh's reply was that of,

'I am not in the mood for any male conversation, it is our night girls, not theirs'

They all agreed and totally ignored them.

The group of lads were miners from the local mine, and Jack who was totally consumed with Niamh and her beautiful face, he was a trainee manager down the local mine.

The band came and they were fabulous. Niamh was desperate to get to the ladies' room, and Jessica accompanied her as they passed the group of lads, Jack bravely spoke out,

'How are you liking the band, girls', as he directed his conversation to Niamh, Niamh completely ignored him, and Jessica followed suit.

As they made their way back to their seats, Jack once again bravely approached their table and directed his conversation towards Niamh,

'I apologise if I have spoken out of turn, I hope I didn't offend in anyway'.

Niamh was stunned and taken back by his bravery and tenacity, and felt a reply was warranted,

'You didn't offend us in anyway, the band is great'.

Jack introduced himself to the girls, and the flow of conversation was cut short as Niamh turned away and that was the end of the conversation. The night came to an end and the girls left the bistro together. Niamh, got a glimpse of Jack waving to her as they got into taxi, she was amused by the whole incident…

Chapter 10

Dylan awoke on this misty morning, in the hope that he would be going home today. It was 7.30 am and the canteen trolley was bustling along giving everyone their morning drink and breakfast.

Mr Roberts the surgeon was due on the ward at 9am and Dylan could not wait, he had his spell in hospital, and a must needed good night sleep in his own bed was long overdue.

The remarkable footsteps along the corridor were that of Mr Roberts who walked briskly towards the ward. Serena had entered the corridor at this time, and spotted him immediately, she rushed towards him with her enquiry,

'Mr Roberts, good morning, will my Dylan be able to come home today?'

He smiled at Serena with his reply,

'Let's see shall we, how are you this morning Dylan, let me check your arm, it is looking rather good, we should be able to do the skin grafting in a few weeks or so, I see no reason why you cannot heal yourself at home for the time being'.

Dylan was relieved and gave Mr Roberts a cheerful smile and spoke.

'Thank you so much doctor for everything. I am so looking forward to going home', as he held Serena's hand.

Serena was beaming and Dylan didn't take long at all to get dressed as Serena assisted him. She was so gentle and careful with Dylan's right arm; it was going to be awkward for him given that he was right-handed.

They arrived in the car park and Serena parked close to the entrance, so Dylan didn't have that far to walk. He was feeling rather strange being in the fresh air but was so happy to feel the misty breeze on his face.

They were both settled in the car and Dylan asked if they could just drive along the coastline, through South Shields, to Whitburn and then Seaburn; the seashores were looking rather magnificent as the clouds began to lift. The sultry spray on the sea gives it that glistening glow to savour. Dylan had his window wound right down and took in the view with a satisfying look on his face.

Serena stopped the car outside the lighthouse, and they decided to have a coffee at the quaint Soothe Café and take in the view for a little while longer. They sat admiring the seashore and watching the ships pass by in the distance. There were also some surfers just about to enter the waters further down the shore.

Dylan turned to Serena with his heartfelt gesture,

'Let's always make up no matter how we might disagree in the future, I just couldn't bear it'.

Serena kissed Dylan getting on the lips and whispered,

'That's a deal my gorgeous husband'.

Dylan looked at Serena and whispered back…

'Gorgeous, a look more like a shaggy dog this morning as he laughed out loud'.

They both laughed for a while and then made their way home to their lovely house, 'The Gables' set by the coastline near South Shields. Dylan had renovated the Georgian style property, it comprised of three bedrooms, a large garden at the rear with a summer house at the bottom of the garden which overlooked the sea front. He had created a pathway with flowered bedding at the sides and two wooden arches which were threaded with flowers.

Serena and Dylan sat in their favourite spot it was in at the rear of the summerhouse which overlooked the promenade as Dylan wanted to take in as much fresh air today as he could. He was told fresh air was a good healer for his arm. As he sat contemplating the past events and was hoping his colleagues were healing too.

He was hoping to get back to work within weeks, but he knew it would be around six weeks. Serena had taken four weeks leave from work, but her father was not too happy about that, as he felt she should be at their practice within a day or two, they agreed to disagree, and Serena won the battle. Her father had made her a partner and she had a say in everything now… ….

Jacqueline telephoned to enquire how Dylan was doing. Serena picked up the receiver and was so happy to hear Jacqueline's voice. She quickly decided to invite her to tea later that day, as she felt a need to have some female support because she was feeling a little jaded from yet another ordeal... Serena always fed off Jacqueline wisdom and strength, it made her feel calmer for some reason.

Dylan asked Serena to invite Colm too, as he wouldn't mind having a chat about what was happening at work. It was settled and Serena would make a casserole for everyone with dumplings, as Jacqueline had given her the recipe months ago and she hadn't tried it out, it was about time she did. A simple fruit dessert would be just the ticket, I think, as she discussed this with Dylan. Dylan was more than happy and nodded his approval.

Colm was going to pop in later to see Dylan, and he was delighted when his mam called him to tell him he had been invited to tea at Dylan's.

Jacqueline decided to call into the wool shop to see Emily, she couldn't believe how the renovations had taken hold. She stood at the front window admiring the display of knitted toys and cushions that were scattered alongside the models, that were wearing the knitted garments. The cross-stitching portraits: a vision of pure perfection, so detailed, with such craftmanship she had never seen before.

As she walked next door to look in the window of the haberdashery store, the display was illuminating with all those sand pebbles that were created into figurines, and the sand pebbled jewellery, Jacqueline gasped with excitement.

Emily spotted her mam outside and went out to greet her, and asked

'Mam what are you doing here?'

'I came down to let you know that Colm and I have been invited for tea so you and Frankie can have the cottage to yourself for tea, there are some steaks in the fridge so help yourselves'.

Emily smiled up at her mam and said,

'Wow, that's great mam, how is Dylan by the way, is he ok?'

Jacqueline replied,

'I think he is doing ok; I think Serena needs a little support she sounded a little needy in her tone of voice, and it is good that Colm is coming too, as he and Dylan will be well into conversation about you know what; the shipyard...

Emily linked her mam into the shops and showed her around and introduced her to the two new members of staff, Jenny the

Junior Assistant, and there was Olivia who was looking after the Haberdashery Store. Olivia was originally from a local store in town, but was keen to come on board and she interviewed so well. Emily was keeping a close eye on the haberdashery store, as Belinda was doing so well in the Wool Shop.

Jacqueline was happy to spend time with her Emily and they talked more about the wedding plans, as Emily was hoping her mam could be able to accompany her that afternoon to the Pavilion where the wedding venue was to take place.

The manager wanted to discuss which coloured sashes Emily would like on the chairs for the reception, and which ornaments she would like on the table settings. Emily had already picked out her pebbled stone creation; it was going to be the centre piece on all the tables, a tree effect with pebbled stoned figurines.

They agreed they both would attend at 2.30pm, Jacqueline was quite looking forward to this. Emily took her mam in the back room and made her a cup of tea with a slice of cake to keep her going for the afternoon as it was going to be busy at the Pavilion.

Jacqueline complimented her Emily on a lovely piece of ginger cake, Emily laughed back at her mam and said,

'It's from the cake shop around the corner', as she giggled back at her mam.

Jacqueline's mind was over thinking as she turned to Emily and asked,

'Why don't you open up a coffee and cake corner next door at the back of the haberdashery store, there is plenty of room'.

Emily looked at the mam with amazement and replied,

'Wow mam, your mind has certainly been working overtime, to come to think of it though, it doesn't seem a bad idea, I will keep that in mind, it will have to be after the wedding though, too much to think about now'.

Jacqueline put her arm around Emily with a prompt reply,

'I think that is a good idea pet'.

They both got up and gathered their belongings and made their way to the car park at the rear of the shop. It was time they were making tracks. It was now 2pm and the venue was around a fifteen-minute drive to get there.

As Emily pulled up at the Pavilion, Jacqueline was taken back with the beautiful structure of the building the stonework on the outside resembled the architecture of ancient Greece, which was rather eye catching.

The front entrance with its prominent stone pillars gives you the sense of a grand entrance, Jacqueline was loving the atmospheric stance that was ruminating around the building. Once inside the marbled reception area they were both greeted by the manager Mr Kitson who was very enthusiastic to say the least; at times he seems overly enthusiastic. Jacqueline's thoughts on the subject were that he had been trained well but was slightly over doing it.

Mr Kitson briskly guided them to the reception room passed the glorious staircase that was mahogany and gold which stood like a mounted haven of supremacy. Jacqueline and Emily glanced at it with a pleasing look on their face.

The reception area with its long Georgian windows and beautiful maroon velvet drapes had set the scene for what must come; a fabulous wedding it would be as Jacqueline took in the sense of the room.

Emily was engaged with Mr Kitson about the table settings, he looked rather confused as he had not heard of beach stoned figurines for the centre pieces of the tables. She quickly took over the matter and was not deterred by Mr Kitson trying to change her mind; she was adamant on the subject, and diverted Mr Kitson to the menu selections and coloured sashes for the chairs which would be lemon as the bridesmaid's dresses were lemon.

The menu was amicably settled, it was to be minestrone soup for starters or alternatively, liver or chicken pate on toast. The main meal was roast beef, and the desert was treacle tart, or strawberry and ice cream.

As they all walked towards the reception area Mr Kitson energetically thanked them both for an interesting afternoon, and he assured them that everything would be in place for the big day.

Jacqueline was first to walk towards the door followed by Emily as they linked each other to the car, Emily turned to her mam with a curious response,

'He was rather over eager wasn't he mam, I sorted him out on the table settings, he was confused about my lovely beach stoned figurines'.

Jacqueline was amused and commented on Mr Kitson's unusual mannerism,

'He sounds like he is not from these parts, he probably hasn't heard of beach stones, it might not have seen a beach for all we know'.

They both howled as they got into the car.

Time was getting on and Colm had arrived home from work just in time to get changed and head to Dylan's. Jacqueline arrived home and called to Colm from the bottom of the stairs.

'We are to be at Dylan's for six Colm'.

He shouted back from the top of the stairs,

'Just getting changed mam, be with you in five'.

It was time for them to head off, Colm started the conversation in the car by saying,

'I hope Dylan is doing ok mam, the other lads in the accident are getting along nicely, they don't blame Dylan for the accident as they know it was human error. They are grateful to him for getting them out so fast, he must know that I will make him know that tonight'.

Jacqueline glanced at her proud son,

'You have grown up so quickly lad, your dad would have been so proud of you'.

Colm answered with a smile,

'I have always been older for my years mam, you know that'.

They had arrived at Dylan's as Serena opened the door to greet them, as she said,

'Dylan is in the summer house at the back Colm, you go through'.

Serena guided Jacqueline to the kitchen and put the kettle on, she wanted a quiet word alone with her, as she spoke lightly.

'We can have five minutes on our own with a quick cuppa'.

Jacqueline was aware that Serena wanted to tell her something, she made herself comfortable and poured the tea.

Serena looked tired and Jacqueline offered to help with the serving of the tea. She told her that it was all sorted as the casserole just needed dishing out, and Jacqueline could help with the laying out in the summerhouse once they had their tea and a quick chat.

Jacqueline asked Serena what was troubling her. She frantically began to tell Jacqueline what was on her mind,

'We are not sleeping together yet, I know he needs time to heal, but I am getting worried that it might not happen, he seems so distant with me!'

Jacqueline held her hand for a moment and said,

'You must stay calm Serena, you both have been through so much these past weeks, it's not surprising feelings and emotions are mixed; I think Dylan will need some time to come to terms with the accident and loss of the baby, and you too pet'.

Serena began to say,

'I thought we were going to be so close when he got home, as we seemed so together in the hospital, I cannot help but worry, but I suppose you are right, I am probably being too inpatient, I just wanted to be held, but I think I might be becoming too selfish'.

Jacqueline immediately responded,

'You are not selfish, you are the most caring person I know, so don't ever think that you just have to slow down a bit, and if you need a cuddle, I am happy to be a substitute for you for now'.

Serena had a tear in her eye, and Jacqueline cuddled her for a moment and then patted her back and said,

'Right let's get this casserole dished out and let us have a lovely tea shall we'.

Serena then smiled and agreed they both went out into the summerhouse where Dylan and Colm were chatting away about the lads at work, and football.

The casserole was delicious, and they all joined in the conversation about the forthcoming wedding, as Dylan kept picking on Colm as he was the best man, it turned out to be a most pleasant evening.

Dylan and Serena said good night to Jaqueline and Colm and as they made their way to the bedroom, Dylan asked Serena to lie down with him, as he spoke in a gentle manner.

'My love, can you just lie down with me and let me hold you on my left side, I know it is not your usual side to the bed, but can we just lie here for a while'.

Serena was over the moon, she felt her prayers had been answered, they lay for some time and Serena could see that Dylan was falling asleep, she stroked his face and kissed him goodnight....

Chapter 11

Today was the day for Jacqueline and Niamh to head to the Deeside College for their first day. Niamh was excited about her new quest at the Teaching College. Jacqueline however was feeling a little apprehensive about her English course.

It was a fine sunny Monday morning, as she opened the curtains to a beaming sun that shone across the sea and the shadowy glimpses scattered along the sandy beach.

As she looked up to the sky, she murmured to herself,

'This is a glorious day of sunshine; I do hope the sun shines on me today'.

Niamh popped her head around Jaqueline's bedroom door and said,

'It's time you were dressed mam, we only have forty-five minutes, its best to get something to eat before we go mam'.

Jacqueline sighed a little and murmured

'To be honest pet, I am not hungry, perhaps a cup of tea and biscuit'.

As Niamh looked up at her mam, and answered,

'Alright mam, I will put the kettle on, don't be long, don't ponder too much mam, you know what you are like when you get in one of your trances'.

Jacqueline smiled back at her daughter with a playful answer,

'Oh, really is that what I do, well I never'.

The light conversation seemed to lift Jacqueline's spirits.

They had finished their light breakfast and headed off to the college, as Niamh pulled up at the college Jacqueline's stomach began to curdle somewhat.

Niamh stared at her mam and asked,

'Is that your stomach rumbling mam, I told you to have some breakfast'.

Jacqueline gave an assertive glance towards Niamh and said,

'Too late now, we are here, let's you go in and get this over with'.

Niamh gave her mam a hug and headed down the other corridor towards the teaching college and Jacqueline headed to the English department where her first class was creative writing.

She strolled down the corridors and through the double doors there were several before she came to her classroom, and there was a hesitant pause before she opened the door as she gasped and muttered to herself,

'What I am doing here, they all look so young, no, this is not for me as she turned away from the door and bumped into a lady who she thought looked in her late 30s, she spoke to Jacqueline and said,

'Hi. Is this the creative writing class, are you joining this class?

Jacqueline found herself saying yes and followed the young lady into the classroom. They both sat down together, and Jacqueline introduced herself. The young lady's name was Louise, and she lived in Cramton 3 miles away, she was also returning to further education.

It was turning out to be a good morning for Jacqueline, not what she had imagined at all, her mood had lifted immensely. Mr Turner the Creative Writing teacher was very enthusiastic, and we were to tackle poetry for our first lesson. The understanding of rhyme, free verse, and conversational poetry, together with the themes and structure of a poem. It was all so fascinating to Jacqueline as she just wrote her poetry without even thinking of rhyme and structure.

The morning flew by, and Jacqueline's mind was buzzing with excitement, she so enjoyed her first morning at college and made a firm friend too. They both headed to the college restaurant and sat down to continue their conversation in relation to how they ended up coming back to college.

Amy was married to a fireman and had two teenage boys. Jacqueline looked confused as she did not look old enough. It turned out that Amy was forty-two years old, she was so flattered, that compliment had cheered her up. She too was feeling so apprehensive about the prospect of returning to education, but she wanted so badly to gain the grades so she could go onto teaching.

Jacqueline really wasn't sure what she wanted from the courses, but it was better than staying at home ruminating about the past and thinking of Declan all the time. She felt that being at college would take her mind of it for a little while at least. Her spirits were lifted so, and she didn't want to lose that, she was determined to make something of herself.

As they sat at their table in deep conversation, Jacqueline felt a pat on her shoulder and looked up and couldn't believe her eyes, it was her old school friend of many years, they had lost touch as Jillian had moved away from the area.

Jacqueline got out of her chair and turned to Jillian and said,

'Oh my! I cannot believe my eyes, my old friend, Jillian, what are you doing here?'

Jillian spoke with a big smile on her face,

'I am in the same class as you, I was at the back and spotted you coming in at the last minute, did you have second thoughts?'

Jacqueline smiled back and said,

'Yes, I did actually, oh! it is so good to see you, when did you move back?'

Jillian sighed and said,

'I moved back two months ago, as I am now divorced so just wanted to get back to my roots'.

Introductions were made and Jacqueline, Amy and Jillian talked more about the course.

The three of them headed back to class and continued the poetry themes for the rest of the afternoon. Jacqueline loved the authors they were studying, Christina Rossetti, Bronte Sisters, these authors were right up her street.

Meanwhile Niamh, was motivated in her class as she got to grips with the keys stages and strategies that were taught in schools, she could see from the offset there was lots to do, and it was going to be so time consuming.

She was committed and motivated and was seated by a young man named Ian who was rather full of himself who came from Durham. Niamh moved quickly away from him as she had spotted a seat vacant at the back of the class and as she sat down, a dark-haired girl approached her and asked if she could sit next to her. Niamh nodded back to her, and they introduced each other. The dark-haired girl with her long curly hair was named Lorretta, she was very bubbly and pointed out that she talked a lot because of her nervousness. Niamh smiled back at her and gave a sign of encouragement,

'No need to be nervous around me, I am a pussy cat'.

Lorretta stared back at Niamh and felt quite at ease with her newfound friend, she hoped they would become friends, and they did.

The week passed by so quickly and there was a lot to take in and study at home too, for this teaching course was not for the faint hearted it was a full-on commitment of your time in class and at home. Niamh and Lorretta met up twice a week in the library to compare notes.

It was Lorretta that seemed to be struggling a bit with what was expected of them for their first week. It was a short exercise they had to complete to recognise figurative language within a sentence, i.e., repetition, alliteration, metaphors, and similes. Niamh told Lorretta that practice makes perfect and not to over think it, she did assist Lorretta a little, but pointed out she could not write it for her.

The week of education for Jacqueline and Niamh ended on a happy note and the weekend was upon them as its time to get those bridesmaids dresses fitted...

The weekend was upon us, and Niamh was ready for a happy distraction the day had come to go and get her bridesmaids dress fitted. A little chaos was happening on this busy Saturday morning for the first hour in the household, and then it settled, and Emily called,

'Order in this house'. Colm smiled with a wink and made his gesture of goodbye,

'Well, I am off to have my morning suit fitted, I will leave you noisy girls to it', as he whistled out the door to be greeted by Aileen and Sara, who were also bridesmaids to make up the numbers.

Emily, Jacqueline, and Niamh were eventually ready to head to the wedding shop the 'Cazalet Elegant Wedding Dresses'. Siobhan Cazalet was the owner of the shop; she was married to a French tailor she met whilst on holiday in Paris. Siobhan was born in Jesmond, her mother was a Geordie, and her father was Irish. Her dream was always to open her own shop in Jesmond and her devoted husband Pierre couldn't let her down with that dream. The shop had only been open a few months and they wanted to impress; no customers were ever disappointed. It was going to be an exciting morning at the Cazalet shop with it quaint French style window.

The Gibson family had arrived, and Jacqueline was so impressed by the display in the window, it had a mannequin dressed in a sequenced lace dress, with a detailed pearled bodice and a long-laced trail with an unusual head piece, shaped like a pyramid. There was a velvet pearled heart shaped trail of sequences embedded in the lace which was rather striking. As the door opened Siobhan greeted them with a class of bubbly and escorted them to the velvet styled Louis French settee. They all gasped with amazement as they soaked in the glorious array of wedding dresses and sublime décor of beautiful orchids.

Siobhan was a tall slim auburn-haired lady; her hair was styled in a French bun; she was impeccably dressed in a pencilled shaped black skirt with a white shirt, and velvet tied bow, it had a diamond in the middle of it. She sat down and discussed Emily's type of dress and her idea of what she was looking for. Siobhan's ideas, however, were starting to rub off on Emily as she entered the dressing room.

Emily tried all the dresses on from lace to satin and silk. As she stepped out in the silk ... it was the one as she looked at herself in the mirror with joyful eyes. It was the silk dress that had a lace bodice to compliment it, it was divine.

Emily made her entrance, and her mam tearfully said,

'Our Emily, that is so gorgeous, I love how the trail sits around you'.

Niamh was in her dressing room and heard the commotion and popped her head out and couldn't hold back with her opinion on such an elegant dress, 'Oh yes, Emily that is you, that truly is you'.

As Niamh tried on her lemon dress, Louisa, Emily's best buddy rushed through the front door gasping! and spoke loudly,

'Sorry, sorry, I am late, stuck in traffic'.

Niamh made her entrance, with the lemon satin dress, with its white daisied waisted sash and long sleeves, it had a triangled cut finish at the cuff, Niamh looked elegant. The head piece was simple with its daisied effect head band which complimented the dress. She was very pleased with the fit of it.

It was Amy who needed some attention, just a few alterations as she had lost a few pounds she had been out on her runs and keeping to a healthy diet, she was obsessed with looking good for the wedding.

Aileen and Sara came out of their cubicles and look magnificent, Emily was so pleased with how the fittings were going.

It was now time for Jacqueline to try her suit on which was a lovely cream colour with a lemon tint to it to compliment the bridesmaid's dresses. It was lovely, a pattern of chained embroidery around the collar of the jacket and around the cuffs which looked quite majestic, Emily loved it and so did Jacqueline. The blouse was pastel yellow colour that went well with the suit. Jaqueline chose a half-moon hat that suited her bob shaped curly hair.

They all sat with their bubbly and was greeted with canopies, chicken pate, and some brie with caramelised onion, which were delicious, Siobhan let them know that it was her French mother-in-law, Celeste, that had made them; the pastry just melted in your mouth it was so good.

Jacqueline turned to Emily and asked,

'You should ask if Celeste wouldn't mind making some for the reception, what do you think pet, I would'.

Emily replied by saying,

'I was thinking the same thing mam; these are too good. We must add them to the menu', I wonder how Frankie and Colm are getting on?'

Colm was the first to come out of his dressing room with his navy-blue morning suit, he looked very dapper. Frankie made his entrance and was a little dismayed as the trousers were a wee bit long, the tailor assured him they would be taken care of that very afternoon so there was nothing to worry about. The wedding wasn't for another three weeks, he was getting excited but nervous at the same time.

They both went for a beer after their fitting, Colm was able to calm Frankie a little, with his dry sense of humour and his laid-back personality. It wasn't long before Frankie was totally relaxed and laughing at Colm's silly jokes.

It had been an eventful day, and they all headed back to the cottage as Jacqueline had prepared a pre wedding buffet for them all.

It was such an unusual warm spring day. The temperature was 17c, and sunny. They could sit in the garden to take in the beautiful shoreline and its shimmering sunshine which slithered across the sandy beach.

Serena and Dylan had arrived as Jacqueline was adamant they should get out and about and enjoy the festivities, they were in good spirits today.

As Jacqueline glanced at them all through the kitchen window, she felt that ache in her stomach, if only Declan were here. She was not going to put a damper on this glorious day and smiled up at the sky and blew a kiss as she felt that Declan was with them in spirit even though his body is laid to rest...

The conversation flowed and the music was on, and as the night draws in and the light breeze whispered across the sea, they all went indoors and said their goodnights...

Chapter 12

Sunday morning had arrived, and Jacquline was always the first to see the light of day, as she headed off to mass. Jacqueline strolled slowly along the beachy head, on this cloudy morning, it's smouldering grey lashing about the seashore. She was overcome with pride and the sense of believing in herself for the first time since Declan's passing.

The parishioners were all gathered outside the church, chatting away merrily. Lydia and Gloria could not help themselves as they approached Jacquline and told her how well the Book Club was going, in fact they boasted away about how they had expanded the class.

Jacqueline gave a wry smile and told them how happy she was for them, and she herself couldn't help herself by saying how well her education was going at Deeside College. Jacqueline was a little annoyed with herself as she went into mass, as it wasn't like her to retaliate in such an arrogant manner. She regretted her outburst and promised herself she wouldn't do that again.

How ironic, the sermon from Fr Donnelly was that on vanity, vanity of vanities…. how true that was as Jacqueline sat and listened carefully to the sermon, and afterwards she decided to go to the coffee morning. The sermon didn't seem to rub off on Gloria and Patricia with their possessiveness with the cake and biscuit making tables. They would give up their ownership of the two top tables.

Fr Donnelly sat with Jacqueline as he looked over to her with a sarcastic look on his face and said,

'They are like two possessive creatures who pounce on their prey and don't give up', as he smirked outright towards their glances.

Jacqueline couldn't have put it better, they both talked awhile about Serena and Dylan and the conversation turned to Niamh and how she was getting on now she was back at college. Fr Donnelly was pleased with everyone's progress. He was disappointed not to have seen Emily this Sunday as the wedding was so close by. Jacqueline was quickly to her defence and told Fr Donnelly that there was important work to be done with the new haberdashery shop, as Emily was appointing a financial manager to oversee the accounts for the two shops. It was an important meeting that was taking place, and it had to be on a quiet day when the shops were closed, it was imperative that Emily should attend. Fr Donnelly gave Jacqueline a nod, which was not that convincing. They said their goodbyes and Jacqueline headed along the beach road where she spotted Bernadette on the beachy rocks with her sketchbook.

She quickened her step and shouted to Bernadette who turned her head towards Jaqueline's direction with a warm smile on her face. They both greeted one another with a friendly hug. Bernadette was the first to speak,

'Where are you off to Jacqueline on this brisk sunny day, are you just out for a Sunday morning stroll, it's definitely the day for a stroll along the beach'.

Jacqueline turned to Bernadette and beckoned her to come forward as she said,

'I have just come from Sunday mass, and yes, it is the day for a stroll; do you fancy a walk along craggy end by the rocks, we can sit and talk for a while and have catch up, it's been an age since I last saw you Bernadette'.

Bernadette was more than happy to go for a walk. As they walked along the beach, Jacqueline remarked on the sea and it's murmuring sound which was rather soothing to listen to. Bernadette was so taken with Jacqueline's remark, they both decided to sit on the sand just to listen to the sea unfold back and forwards with its waves of comfort. It was music to your ears; they sat for a moment and savoured that sensation of calm and tranquillity.

'So, Bernadette, how is the job at the art museum going, are you enjoying it'.

Bernadette smiled back at Jacqueline and said,

'Oh, it's great, I am so lucky to have been chosen, there were so many candidates, I feel so happy they chose me'.

Jacqueline put her hand on Bernadete's arm and responded by saying,

'They are lucky to have you pet, you are so talented, don't put yourself down girl'

Bernadette liked Jacqueline a lot, and as she and Colm were getting rather close, she hoped one day Jacqueline would be her Mother-in-law. She wasn't going to say anything about that as Colm was the one to instigate such further developments on that score. Bernadette was quite happy that Colm was the strong one in the relationship, and she would be guided by his next move. If last night was anything to go by, she felt that they had moved on rather quickly as they had made love for the very first-time and she was ecstatic about the situation.

Jacqueline had noticed a glow in Bernadette's cheeks and delicately asked if she was seeing Colm this Sunday at all, as Colm was not giving anything away to his dear mother.

Bernadette replied with a cautious respond.

'Yes, Colm and I are stretching this afternoon actually'.

Jacqueline was quick to respond by asking Bernadette to come to lunch as she was hoping she may get some more insight to their relationship.

Bernadette was delighted to accept the invitation to lunch as she was so looking forward to seeing Colm today after their special night together.

After a long stroll along craggy end, they were both in need of a refreshing drink of lemonade and as they entered the cottage they were greeted by Colm at the back door.

As Colm and Bernadette's eyes met, Jacqueline knew instantly that their relationship had hit the most important level of courtship as the intimacy was glaring out on their beaming faces. Jacqueline made herself scarce by pointing out she was to get Sunday lunch on as Colm and Bernadette sat in the garden just staring lovingly at each other.

Finally, they were completely alone, and Colm got up to put his arms around Bernadette and passionately kissed on and murmured in her ear,

'I love you so much, you beautiful creature'.

Bernadette nervously murmured in his ear.

'I love you more, you gorgeous creature'.

Jacqueline caught a glimpse of them through the kitchen window, she quickly moved away with a joyous smile on her face.

Emily entered the kitchen, her meeting was over, and she was so thankful things were going to be so great with the new venture of both shops, in fact, they were thriving. She had just had a new safe delivered that very week which was placed at the back of the haberdashery shop, it would be sufficient for both shops, as he would store all takings in there overnight.

Niamh came downstairs to join everyone for Sunday lunch, she too, had noticed a glow in Bernadette's cheeks, and a rather starry-eyed Colm as she look pensively at her brother. They tucked into their delicious roast beef and Yorkshire puddings...

Niamh got into a conversation quickly with her brother Colm and Bernadette by asking if he had any plans for the rest of the day and how things were going with them.

Colm spluttered a little and put his fork down on the table and quietly replied by saying that they were both doing their usual sketching on the beach as they always do, and everything was going just great with the sketching. He got up quickly from the table with a hurried response,

'It's about time we were down at the beach', as he ushered Bernadette out the door.

Emily turned to Niamh and asked,

'What is going on with them two?'

Niamh turned to her sister with a prominent reply,

'I think something more is going on if you asked me'.

Jacqueline agreed with that assumption and went on further to say that she was so happy for them both as they are so well suited. Emily and Niamh totally agreed, although Niamh couldn't believe it herself. She was always of the view her dear brother was going to be a late starter; it appears not as they all smiled at one another.

The conversation turned to education as Niamh was asking her mam how she was getting on with the creative writing so far. Jacqueline was overjoyed with her newfound learning and was keen to know how Niamh was doing.

As Niamh sat back in her chair, she told her mam and Emily that the course was going to be harder than she had anticipated so she will be spending more time studying and more time at the library. She was not going to fail this course. Jacqueline was relieved to hear that Niamh was focused and it wouldn't be that long before she would be teaching.

They all turned the conversation on its head by getting back to the wedding and all its arrangements. There wasn't that much to do now as the wedding was only two weeks away and Niamh wanted to talk about the hen party.

She encouraged Emily to get the sashes made and she would sort the venue out, as the Front View at the beachy head was ideal for a hen party as they had a big dance floor. Niamh would get the show on the road, with balloons and mini gift bags for all, she wanted to make a great night for her dear sister, after all, it isn't every day you get married.

It was lovely afternoon as the three of them carried on with the conversation out in the garden with their deserts of Strawberries and Ice Cream. As the afternoon went on it began to get chilly that Northeast breeze was picking up somewhat.

As they made their way into the cottage the front doorbell rang, and it was Sara she had come to visit her sister Jacqueline to find out how everything was going at college. She had her cocker spaniel with her, Brodie as they had been out for a good walk. Brodie loved his walks along the beach, he loved the sea waves and would jump in and out of them for some reason. Sara believed he just loved the movement of the folding waves; it was almost as if he was trying catch one and wouldn't give up.

Jacqueline was anxious how things were with John and the business; everything was going well Sara told her and she had good news of her own. She had been promoted to clinical supervisor and was so elated about it; she loved her job in the hospital.

A celebration night was held, and they drank a few glasses of wine and reminisced about their childhood and their aspirations. They both laughed at each other as Sara turned to Jacqueline and said,

'Can you remember your ideal job you were going to have our Jacqueline'.

Jacqueline laughed out loud with a sinister response,

'Oh yes, an Air Hostess, as if '.

Sara yours was a Beautician, can you remember that.

The night went by so quickly and it was bedtime......

As Emily lay in her bed, she questioned herself about the alarm at the shops and the safe, it was all locked up, she checked twice.

'Why I am repeating myself in my sleep, go to sleep' she said to herself.

As she was sleeping there were three young men outside the shop at midnight. Alfie who was the ringleader, he was a mechanic who had been in prison, he was a master of cracking safes. He learned a lot in prison and became so efficient with new ideas on how to crack a safe without anyone even noticing it had been broken into.

He had defined a file like knife with a special kink in it so you could easily lodge it behind the dial of a safe, it could decipher the code on any safe. It was also handy for taking out seals on windows, they would re-seal it before the three of them left the premises.

Ronnie had the sealant in his haversack, he was the window man who knew how to do a good job on re-sealing the window.

Stewart was the driver of the van; he was to stay in the van and keep a look out for anyone passing by.

The three men had been watching the shops for weeks and were very happy to have a caught a glimpse of the safe arriving that very week. They were ready to go ahead... that night... It was the end of the month, and their way of thinking was it would be the ideal time to crack the safe as it should have enough cash in there.

Alfie disarmed the alarm from the outside which transferred to the indoor alarm, he managed that without any fuss at all. Ronnie was ready to get in at the back window and un-sealed the window it was done quickly.

Alfie made his way to the safe, it didn't take him long to decipher the code as he placed his filing knife behind the key code which sat nicely.

It was a delicate job, and it took thirty minutes, and he was in. There was £1,000 in cash, Ronnie was happy with that and some jewellery which looked non-significant to him. A collection of jewellery that Emily had placed in the safe was necklaces for the bridesmaids and their head pieces. Ronnie was only interested in the cash. He delicately placed the safe door back in its place and it clicked nicely, it was if no one had ever been in the safe at all.

They were out the premises in a flash and Ronnie re-sealed the window. As they both got in car, they couldn't believe there was a £1,000 in the safe, it was the takings for both shops and the staff wages, and a large amount of petty cash, it was their lucky night…

Alfie carefully climbed up the ladder and reconnected the alarm without any issue at all. He was surprised that they hadn't fitted a sophisticated alarm system, as he wickedly smiled at himself as he got into the van with the cash in his haversack.

It was time for them to make a quick getaway. Stewart drove off with speed, and they all roared with joy. It was to be a three-way split, but Alfie had other ideas he persuaded them to let him hold on to the money and they all agreed that would be the case…

Chapter 13

It was a dismal Monday morning, as the mist and rain gathered across the sea. Emily lay on her bed and rubbed her eyes aggressively as began talking to herself.

'I must wake up, I must get myself in the bathroom, it's a busy day, banking to get done' as she gave out a weary sigh.

'Oh, what the heck, I will let Belinda take charge for once, she is doing a great job, I have too much to do'.

She sprang out of bed and hopped into the bathroom. Colm was already in there and she became impatient as he whistled away and ignored her every plea. It was Jacqueline who came to her rescue and shouted with a firm voice.

'You get out of there dear lad; you are not too old to be tanned!'

Colm opened the door with his laid-back attitude,

'What's all the fuss about, I am finished now', as he winked at his mam and patted her on the back. Jacqueline gave him a stern stare but with an amusing smile on her face at the same time.

Everyone was hustling along to get ready for their day ahead. Jacqueline was excited about her start of the week, as the lectures today were all fiction. Jane Eyre, Charlotte Bronte. Ann Bronte, The Tenant of Wildfell Hall. As she dressed herself with her thoughts of literature, she couldn't believe how she was transforming into something completely different to that of a mother, a wife and a home keeper.

She felt a sense of adventure and liberation in her soul that seemed to be driving her towards the unknown, it was a little scary, but she was so excited about the learning process and simply put the scary part out of her mind.

She had awoken with such excitement that morning and smiled at Declan's picture on the bed side table. She picked it up and kissed it and said,

'I hope you approve my love; I wish you were here to see me transform into something new'.

She strolled out of the bedroom and down the stairs with a kind of serene look on her face. Niamh followed her down the stairs and turned to her mam with a puzzled response,

'You look different today mam, what is it? I cannot put my finger on it, but you look different'.

Jacqueline smiled at her daughter and said,

'It might be the earrings I have on; I have not worn them for some time'.

Niamh, smiled warmly at her mam, and agreed,

'Yes, that must be it'.

Niamh was surprised to see them on her mam, as she hadn't worn them since her dad had passed. She stared at her mam for a moment and her thoughts were that her mam had turned a corner, and I too, must turn the corner completely so I can get rid of my vulnerability and insecurities.

She was annoyed with herself at times, as she felt that the trauma had gone on enough in her thoughts and mind; she was going to wash them thoughts away for good. I will not let that horrible man that attacked me get into my head no more as she walked out the door behind her mam.

Emily was scurrying away to get herself already for the off. As she arrived at the shop Belinda had already opened the shops. Jenny and Olivia were just arriving. It was unusual for Emily to be this late, she was the one who was in the shop first and would get everything set up before anyone arrived.

The wedding was taking so much of her time, and she was feeling a little anxious and stressed about everything, but the nevertheless Emily would always hide it, and put on her best face on and power away with her instructions for the day.

As everyone assembled themselves in their positions in the shop, Emily called Belinda over and told her she could oversee the banking. Belinda was so surprised but very happy to do so. Emily pointed out to Belinda that she should take the takings, petty cash, and wages to the bank directly, as she had not the time late Friday afternoon to her annoyance. She didn't like leaving the monies in the safe over the weekend, but it was a one off and the safe and buildings were very secure or so she thought.

Emily handed the keys to Belinda, and she opened the safe as she looked in and pulled out the stoned pebbled necklaces to her horror there was nothing else in the safe. She shouted rather loudly to Emily!

'Emily! There is no money in the safe! Just the necklaces!'

Emily frantically made her way to the safe with an anxious reply,

'Let me have a look, let me see, the monies must be here'.

As she turned to Belinda and asked,

'Was the safe secure, did you notice anything untoward? Was the door secured enough?

Belinda replied,

'It was intact, I put the combination in, and it opened as it should, I don't understand?'

As Emily turned to Belinda with a puzzled expression on her face as she spoke out,

'Neither do I, this is bizarre, check the back door, check the windows, check everything in this shop, turn everything over'.

They spent hours going through the shop until eventually Emily telephoned her Aunt Aileen to tell her the devastating news. Aileen got into her car and arrived twenty minutes later. As she rushed into the shop, she also checked everywhere with Emily and spoke directly,

'Emily you must call the police and the insurance company, let's see if they can decipher all this, it's a mystery; there doesn't seem to be a break-in, I just don't understand how the monies could get out of the safe unless someone had the combination'.

They looked at one another rather suspiciously, and Emily sparked off with a sturdy comment,

'Aunt that cannot be possible! I trust everyone in this shop and the combination is only known by yourself, myself, and Belinda. The written combination is locked in the drawer, and I have the key'.

Aunt Aileen took back what she said,

'I wasn't accusing anybody at all, I was just thinking out loud, let's just get the police and insurance assessor in so they can get to the bottom of this dreadful situation pet'.

The police arrived on the scene thirty minutes later, DS Richards and DC Cramer were the policeman who had a look around and checked everywhere. They could not find evidence of a break in and advised everyone, and they would be interviewed under caution. The whole staff were all shaken up over this. Emily was inconsolable, as she felt responsible somehow. She went over and over her movements since Friday night and couldn't pinpoint anything at all. She was completely bamboozled.

'How the hell can someone get monies out of the safe who don't know the combination?'

Emily was feeling distraught about everything, and Aunt Aileen came to the rescue and supported her niece by saying,

'Don't' worry about anything I will recompense the safe monies for now until the insurance company reimburse you'.

Emily gave a tearful response to that,

'Oh, Aunt that means the premiums will go up, oh! how could this happen at this time, the wedding is 12 days away!'

Aunt Aileen put her arm around Emily and spoke out with conviction,

'Now you listen here, it is not the end of the world, we will sort this mess out and you must not get yourself in such a state, leave it to me'.

Emily hugged her aunt with warm gesture,

'What would I do without Aunt'.

Aileen replied in a rather joking manner by saying,

'You probably be in the knitting circle down at the centre I suppose, just kidding my pet, a bit of humour goes a long way to break the ice'.

Emily couldn't be annoyed with her aunt as she did have a wicked sense of humour and would always announce something completely out of the ordinary, she did at times get people's backs up, but she had big shoulders, it just bounced off her.

DS Richards turned to DC Cramer and told him to check everyone's belongings, and he informed the staff that he would need all their names and addresses, and he would be searching their homes. The whole staff look alarmed, but DC Cramer assured them that it was police procedure nothing to worry about.

Meanwhile the insurance assessor had arrived to pour more alarming news on to Emily by informing her that the claim for the monies in the safe would not be honoured as there is no evidence of a break-in or forced entry into the building.

Emily turned to her Aunt Aileen and said,

'This is my worst nightmare, I just cannot fathom this at all, I really cannot'.

Aileen was flabbergasted at the news! She sat in the back and put the kettle on and sat Emily down as they went through everything with a fine-tooth comb.

The Police had conducted their enquiries, but nothing was found, but they were going to keep an open mind and will need to speak to everyone later. As they got into their police cars, DS Richards turned to DC Cramer and said,

'I have never come across a burglary that wasn't a burglary?'

'It must be an inside job; it cannot be anything else. We will have to go back to the gov with this as I think this is a surveillance job, don't make any plans for tonight lad'.

DC Cramer was not happy, and his response was rather abrupt!

'Oh, I see, that's my date out of the window tonight then!'.

DS Richard responded with his cold eyes.

'That's the nature of the job lad, you have to be on hand any time, any place'.

The whole day was a disaster, and they called it a day early. They all left the shop with a worried look on their face, even though they had not done anything wrong.

Aileen turned to Emily with a comforting gesture,

'I will follow you home pet, as I was going call and see my mam later anyway'.

Emily was pleased, as she felt she needed her hand held when she lets the family know of the awful events of today.

Jacqueline and Niamh were home, as it was 4.30pm in the afternoon. They were both stunned at the news! As Jacqueline looked at her daughter Emily, with her pale exterior, she embraced her with a soft reply.

'Don't get yourself in a state your aunt has sorted this and that's the end of it, so don't dwell on this, do you hear me'.

Emily looked up at her mam and as she spoke her voice seem to echo a kind of hope that might come out of this situation.

'You and Aunt Aileen are like two peas in a pod you always come up with the same positive attitude when things are grim, I am going upstairs to have a lie down mam'.

Aileen followed Jacqueline and Niamh to the kitchen. They all sat down and put their heads together trying to find a solution. Jacqueline wondered if they should call Serena, as she has investigators in her line of work, lawyers always have investigators. They all decided it was worth a shot, as they couldn't come to any solution over this at all.

Serena arrived after work and was pleased to offer her assistance. She had just the right man for this a very experienced forensic investigator, Jake, and she would call him. She turned to them all and said,

'If anyone can get to the bottom of this Jake can, I assure you'.

Jacqueline and Aileen were hopeful of this outcome as they too were worried about Emily, and this needed to be resolved sooner rather than later.

The next day Jake arrived at the shop and brought all his equipment with him. He had two vintage hand-held magnifying glasses with curled horns that tilted in every angle which was fascinating. As he began his quest to solve this mystery. He put the magnifying glass behind the combination which slipped down nicely; it was a slender piece of equipment, and he put the other tilting magnifying glass above so he could see if there were any indentations at all that implied the combination had been tampered with.

He asked Emily to assist him by grabbing the camera, she would have to get up onto the stair ladder which was a wooden robust ladder with a large standing area, she could take the photo without any bother. Jake told Emily to take at least three pictures from different angles.

When the task was done Jake turned to Emily saying,

'This safe has certainly been tampered with, it looks like whoever did this, knew what they were doing'

Emily was so relieved and so was everyone else, but the fact of the matter was how the hell did they get in. Jake responded by saying,

'The same way as they tampered with the safe a delicate piece of equipment and wearing gloves; I would think there would be more than one involved here, I can notify the police if you would like'.

Emily gratefully said yes, as she knew Jake would be able to inform the police more thoroughly than she could. He telephoned DCI Steele who was most interested in these findings, as he was aware that there was a gang who broke into various buildings without a trace years ago. He will send his detectives along immediately.

Jake was asked if he would like to do some freelance with the police. Jake smiled at him with his head tilted,

'I have been asked many times, but I am so busy with my freelance for the law firms at the moment, but I will bear you in mind, this was a favour for a friend of the family'.

The problem was who are the culprits, DCI Steele had two in mind, he knew Alfie would be one of them as he was well known to him. He would call on his so-called friends, Stewart and Ronnie to ascertain his whereabouts. He was not too hopeful they would cough up, but it was worth a shot.

DCI Steele arrived at Stewart's home, the driver of the vehicle. His mother informed the DCI that he was down the snooker hall. She abruptly shouted after them,

'He has done nothing wrong, leave him alone!'

As the DCI arrived at the snooker hall, he informed DS Richards to watch the back door just in case he decides to bolt!

He made his entrance into the snooker room and there were quite a few men playing snooker, he browsed each table and then spotted Stewart on the back table and put his hand on his shoulder and spoke quietly in his ear.

'Can I have word in your ear lad, do you remember me'.

Stewart looked up nervously at DCI Steele, oh, he remembered DCI Steele back in 1966 (3 years ago) when he collared him and sent him away for twelve months. Stewart was confused, how could he know about the burglary it was perfect, no fingerprints, he had nothing on him. He gave a naïve look towards the DCI, as he knew his mam would vouch for him if he needed an alibi.

After his interview with the DCI, he let Stewart go on a caution, but he was told not to leave the area. The DCI would be in touch shortly; this left a shiver down Stewart's back as he left the police station.

DCI Steele and DS Richards followed him out and got into the police car, they were convinced he was involved he looked nervous, twitchy. His naivety was not convincing. The problem is they have no witnesses. They would need to put a notice in the paper and get it on the news, someone must have seen something.

It wasn't long before a call came in from a man leaving the pub around the corner that night and he noticed a white van with three men sitting in it, they got out and had a conversation before going around the back of the shops. The man explained that he would come in and look at some mug shots, he did get a look at the driver clearly, not so much the other two though.

After looking through the mug shots, there was an identity parade held, and he put his shoulder on Stewart.... Things were now getting interesting, as DCI Steele clapped his hands and said,

'We got him, we just need the safe breaker'……

Chapter 14

The sun shone so brightly on this Wednesday morning and the coastline streets breathed in that sultry salty air. It was 7.30am and the shopkeepers along the beachy road were already putting out their billboards, especially the coffee shops and café's as they were getting ready for the mid-week morning workers rush hour that started at 8.00am.

Emily too was parking up outside the haberdashery shop, as she walked towards the front entrance, she spotted Olivia and Jenny in deep conversation. They were still trying to get over the devastation and humiliation of the burglary. Olivia had told Jenny how her father was up in arms when the police turned up to search the house. He soon calmed down when the constable explained that it was just procedure no one was getting arrested.

Jenny was not too pleased herself as she was the outspoken one and found it hard to take in. She didn't hold back when the police searched her home. She lived with her mam and sister, as her father had passed away when she was young with a blood disorder. Her personality was very sharp and direct being the oldest in the household as her mam was quite shy and timid.

They all entered the shop, and Emily consoled them both by giving them a slight rise in their wages due to the upset and humiliation of it all. They were both happy with that outcome. One shilling and sixpence was not a bad rise at all, as they smiled at each other.

Olivia put the kettle on for everyone before the shop opened, they always had a cuppa first thing. As they sat in the back of the shop Jenny enquired about the culprit they had in custody.

All Emily could tell them is that DCI Steele was interviewing a man, and they think that more men were involved. She assured Jenny and Olivia that everything would get back to normal soon and they were not concern themselves anymore.

DCI Steele arrived in the interview room he was just waiting on the prisoner Stewart to be brought up from the cells. As Stewart entered the room he shouted!

'I want a Solicitor; I am entitled to a Solicitor! I know about that!'

DCI Steele responded sternly,

'Yes, Stewart, your brief is on his way, so why don't we just chat a bit before he gets here'.

Stewart shuffled in his chair and twitched away rubbing his hands up and down stuttering away,

'I have nothing say, I don't know anything'.

DCI got out of his chair and raised his voice,

'Listen here lad, you have been identified in the line up, so don't tell me you know nothing! I know you do, so why don't you make your life easier lad by just telling us how many accomplishes were there; I am sure you didn't do this alone lad?'

Stewart looked up at the ceiling and didn't say a word.

His brief had arrived a Mr Kemble, who was tall sandy haired man. He dressed impeccably in a navy-blue suit and his silk tie. He swaggered in with such arrogance and said,

'I need to have a word with my client please, we will need thirty minutes at least'

DCI Steele replied sarcastically,

'You have ten minutes.'

Mr Kemble took his client's instructions and asked him not to lie to him. Stewart looked alarmed for a moment and didn't reply straight-away. His thoughts were frantically trying to work out what to say. He eventually spoke to his solicitor.

'I was only driving, I didn't do anything, I didn't take the money! it was Alfie and Ronnie who did the burglary and Alfie has the money'.

Mr Kemble instructed his client to divulge this information to the police as he would get a much lesser sentence as he wasn't involved in the burglary. He had only one conviction in the past and Mr Kemble was convinced that he would only be sentenced for six months, and he could be out in three months. If he does not co-operate with the police, they could make life difficult for him.

Stewart sat back in his chair and pondered on the information he had just received; he had come to a decision he was not going to prison for years so he will take Mr Kemble's advice on this and co-operate with the police.

DCI Steele stood in the doorway with Mr Kemble and shook his hand and said,

'It is nice doing business with you Mr Kemble'.

Mr Kemble responded by saying,

'If he hadn't been identified in the identity parade, it would be a different story'.

DCI Steele turned to Mr Kemble with his pertinent answer,

'I am sure it would be a different story', as he strolled passed Mr Kemble with his eyebrow raised as he glanced back at him.

It was time to make the search immediate in the finding of Alfie as DCI Steele was sure he would be making his way either by train or ferry. He would alert all involved and hopefully by the end of the day he would have Alfie behind bars. His commitment and work ethic were to work around the clock, and he would not stop until he had him in custody.

Meanwhile Alfie said goodbye to his mam, not letting on where he was going, just that he had a job offer over the river, which was of course a lie. His mam had no idea what was happening but was happy to see her son off thinking what a good lad he was. He did in fact look after his mam in his own way, but his nifty fingers would always get the better of him.

He made his way to the ferry, and over his shoulder was black and white haversack; the £1,000 was neatly tucked at the bottom part of the haversack.

The ferry was crowded it was a busy crossing so Alfie was pleased about that as he wouldn't be noticed that much. He quickly boarded the ferry and tucked himself away at the back in a quiet corner and pushed his flecked brown hair into his black and white flat cap.

Unfortunately for him DS Richards and DC Cramer were already on board. The DC made his way up the stairs to the upper deck. DS Richards scoured the lower deck he knew Alfie's profile so it shouldn't be long before he found him. Alfie had not spotted him as he had his cap downwards.

DS Richards noticed someone crunched in the corner looking rather suspicious. He went over and patted him on the shoulder and Alfie looked up with horror. He tried to tussle his way out to no avail. DS Richards was an expert on getting the handcuffs on so quickly. DC Cramer arrived on the scene and they both escorted him off the ferry which stopped at the first stop at North Shields where DCI Steele was eagerly waiting.

It wasn't long after that Ronnie the third man was picked up. Alfie was more than happy to grass on him, as his thoughts were,

'If I am going down, so is he'

It had been a successful collar for all involved and DCI Steele for the first time in his career told the lads that the drinks were on him, as all the lads looked on with astonishment. Everyone turned up for their free drink.

The DCI telephoned Emily to give her the good news before venturing off to the pub, 'The Top Hat' the policeman's local pub where they all let off steam and celebrated their success.

Emily was so excited about the news, she wept with joy, as she turned to her mam.

'Mam, they have caught the culprits and not only that they have recovered the £1,000.00'.

Jacqueline put her arms around Emily shouting!

'I knew it would turn out well pet, I knew DCI Steele would sort this one, he is a stickler for detail and a stickler for getting the job done'.

Niamh came through the front door after her long session at the library and was so happy about the news as she joined in with the conversation.

'I think we three should head to the pub; I will call Aunt Aileen and Aunt Sara, let's make it a family affair'.

Colm interrupted Niamh and responded,

'Hey sis, what about me, am I not family?'

Niamh glanced at Colm with a warm smile on her face,

'Aw I thought you would be out with Bernadette, but if you and Bernadette would like to come along, that would great our Colm'.

He looked surprised at Niamh's response; it was time they were seen with the family more often.

Colm was picking Bernadette up at 7.00pm, they were going to try ten pin bowling out for the first time, but Bernadette was more than happy to go to the pub and spend time with Colm's family.

They all met up at, 'The Swan', as they hadn't been there for good while and it was a big celebration.

As they entered the pub, it was buzzing with rock and roll music tonight, 'The Dragetts', were playing. It was rather large pub with three sections to it, and it had extra decking outside which was almost on the beach.

The owners had extended the sitting arrangements as they were having regular bands almost every night and there was the big quiz night on a Wednesday.

Niamh suggested they go out to the decking as there was amble seating for everyone, and it wasn't that cold, they were all too excited to be cold.

Jacqueline took charge and ordered all the drinks, she was happy to get the first round in as she was so relieved for her daughter Emily, and now the wedding plans can get started without any more drama.

They put their glasses together and said at the same time,
'Cheers everyone'.

Niamh stood up and made a speech,
'Raise your glasses once more to the forthcoming hen party which is in two days'.

Everyone Cheered, and as they did, the whole pub cheered with them.

Bernadette was fitting in nicely with the family, and Jacqueline was pleased, she was beginning to really take to Bernadette, with a warm, caring personality.

Emily chatted away about the success of the burglary, and it was decided that they would have an updated alarm that was full proof and a new safe. She got up to go to the ladies' room and noticed Jack at the bar with his friends, he waved to Emily over to him and she responded.

As they stood at the bar, Niamh was shocked that Emily took time to speak to him, as she made it quite clear the last time when she met Jack that she was not interested, or was she? It was too soon for Niamh to contemplate an attraction in her head, but in her heart, she was attracted to Jack's stance. It was the way he held himself, and his witty personality which was attractive. She looked nervously across at Emily; they were talking for a such a long time.

Eventually Emily made her way to the ladies' room, and Niamh quickly followed on as she dying to know what they talked about.

As they both sat in the sitting area of the ladies' room; 'The Swan', was the only pub that had a dressing/makeup room for the ladies to freshen up which was spacious and eloquently decorated with pastel colours and large mirrors.

Emily looked on rather nonchalantly,

'We were just talking about the celebrations, and my forthcoming wedding'.

Niamh impatiently pushed her sister and raised her voice,

'Oh, come on, you must have been talking about something else, you were there talking for ages!'

Emily kept her cool and said to her sister,

'Of course we talked about you, he was eager to know more about you, and I told him you were sweetest and most generous person you would ever wish to meet; he was eager to know more about you, and I didn't divulge anything that happened at university, no I didn't mention the assault'.

Niamh sighed and looked at her sister before saying,

'I don't think this is a good idea sis, I don't think I want to get to know him just yet'.

Emily put her arm around her sister,

'Just take it slow Niamh, baby steps, trust me, he seems such a nice guy, I think you should give him a chance'.

They both went back to their table, and Jack couldn't take his eyes of Niamh and when the band began their second session, he spotted his chance to ask Niamh to dance as there was a great dance area in the pub and everyone was dancing.

Jack was a good dancer, as they danced the twist, Niamh was starting to enjoy herself too much. After the dance was over Jack asked Niamh if she would like a drink, and she seemed a little tentative but in the end she accepted.

They both sat on the stools by the bar and chatted about their hobbies. Jack was a keen walker and like to get out in the countryside, he was always on his bicycle. He loved the outdoors, simply because he was underground all day at the mine at Dunston Colliery.

Niamh explained to Jack that her late father was a manager down the mine, he looked stunned and responded,

'Oh, wow! Your father is Declan Gibson, I have seen his portrait on the memory board, he has a plaque that was donated to him for his services; the men are always talking about what a great manager he was and how he looked after his men'.

Niamh choked back the tears and quivered,

'He was'

The compassion and the mature way that Jack consoled Niamh was rather touching and they changed the subject to Niamh and her studies and her pursuits and passions in life.

Niamh energetically began by saying that she was passionate about teaching and helping others and she was hoping to be a good horse rider one day, she was getting there with the help from Serena. She went on to say that she loved to play tennis too in her spare time.

Jack jumped in and said,

'Aw well lass, I play a bit of tennis myself, so we should head to the tennis courts sometime soon'.

Nimah was animated, 'Why not, let's do that'.

Jacqueline kept glancing over to them and was worried a little, she was hoping that Niamh was not feeling too vulnerable and didn't jump in too quickly.

Emily reassured her mam,

'Mam, he is a nice lad, he seems mature for his age; I told Niamh baby steps, look at her mam, she hasn't looked that happy since the assault'.

Jacqueline agreed reluctantly, and they went back to the conversation about the wedding, everything was organised and there was nothing to worry about now.

As the night ended, Jack said goodnight to Niamh outside the pub, and grabbed her hand in a flamboyant fashion, he had such away about him as he took Niamh's hand and kissed it,

'It's been an absolute great night; I have enjoyed your company Niamh; may I ask for your telephone number to arrange our tennis match?', as he eagerly awaited her reply, he put his hand out so Niamh could write it on his hand.

Niamh always carried a pen with her and went inside her bag to achieve it,

'There you are Jack, I am busy most of the time studying, but Saturday afternoon is a good time to spend a few hours on the tennis court'.

Jack was delighted with the response, and everyone was waiting in the taxi for Niamh. As she sat in the taxi, she looked back at Jack and waved.

Her mind and thoughts were so mulled with excitement and confusion, her mam was right, she was feeling vulnerable, but in a nice way.

As she slept in her bed, her dreams seem to be serene and calm, it was a sensation she hadn't felt for such a long time….

Chapter 15

Serena lay in bed as Dylan whistled away in the bathroom. It had been an evening of mixed feelings and emotions which flowed like a river. It turned out to be a night of kiss and tell as they were both open when unleashing their thoughts and fears of ever having another baby. It didn't take long for them to become passionate, and the passion continued throughout the night...they had been having several nights like these... ...

As they lay all night wrapped up in each other. It was 6am before Serena awoke first, she turned on her side and sat up. As she looked out of the window and happily muttered to herself...

'We didn't close the curtains, oops... at least we are not overlooked as she laughed out loud', such laughter awoke Dylan from his deep sleep...

'What are you laughing about beautiful', as he grabbed her around the waist and pulled her back into bed,

Serena snuggled into his chest,

'We didn't close the curtains love' said she,

Dylan's left eyebrow lifted, and he gave a coy reply,

'And who is watching, we are not overlooked'. Their garden was heavily bedded with magnificent shrubbery and that beautiful oak tree that stood so tall and proud in the background.

Dylan turned to Serena

'Hen night tonight pet, has Niamh sorted Emily's big night, do you know where you are all going?'

Serena smirked at Dylan as she pressed her hand on his cheek and whispered,

'As if I would tell you, no way love, no chance'.

Dylan laughed out loud and responded by saying,

'Frankie's best mate Ian has it all sorted for the stag night, he is going to be a great best man that is for sure, what a character'.

As they sat on the bed and caressed each other, as if their souls were combined with the joy and the pain they had endured. Dylan lay himself against her and kissed her passionately and then whispered in her ear,

'Love you forever my beautiful wife, as he got up and blew her kiss, see you later beautiful'.

Serena sat for a moment and realised how lucky she was to have Dylan, who strengthened her every time they touched.

She sprung from the bedside and went to the bathroom, she was washed and dressed in no time; as she smiled at herself in the mirror and muttered, 'It's going to be a good day'.

Emily was rushing around like a headless chicken, as she wanted to finish working at the store at 4pm to give Niamh a hand with the preparations for the hen night. They both needed to get to the Caster's bar to get set up. Emily had no idea what Niamh had prepared? She was rather excited about it.

As the day passed by so quickly, Emily made her way to the bar and met up with Niamh. There was van parked outside with a sign on the side of it saying, 'party accessories.'

'So, sis, what accessories are they I wonder?'

Niamh candidly winked at her sister,

'Wait and see, as she raised her right eyebrow'.

As the van started to unload, there were balloons with gold coloured pencil so eloquently drawn across the centre of them saying, 'Hen Party' and very colourful sashes illustrating, 'hens', and one for the bride. They unloaded what looked like lampshades with sparklers on top of them?

Emily looked stunned by it all, as her sister went on to say,

'There is more inside'.

Niamh took Emily in the back room of the bar where she had her bride's outfit which consisted of a white tu tu dress, not too short, as she knew Emily wouldn't go for it. Niamh guided Emily to the staff's changing lockers and told her to shut her eyes. As the locker door opened Niamh shouted out,

'Voila!'

Emily was star struck, as she stared into the tu tu and those white tights! Oh! a glittering tiara and a special sash; with a bright pink emblem on it stating the words, 'bride' with its white and pink ribbons.

Emily laughed and cried at the same time and choked out her words,

'Wow, our Niamh, you certainly brought out your creative side', she couldn't stop laughing and crying. They hugged each other until they couldn't breathe...

You will wear it our Emily', as Niamh looked a little worried, as she might have gone too far with the tu tu…

Emily put her hands around Niamh's neck and responded with a kiss on her cheek.

'One night only, ooh what a night we are going to have'.

Jacqueline had prepared buffet food for her daughter's big night.

The Broadstairs soul band were booked for later that evening.

As Emily tried her outfit on to see how it looked, she was quietly surprised it didn't look too bad at all, as she felt like a princess which was rather pleasing to her.

Frankie and Ian were getting ready for their stag night, which was to take place near the coast road, which was set back, but you couldn't take your eyes of this artistic building as it was shaped like a ship.

The architecture and detail that was portrayed in this magnificent building was so eye-catching. It was finished off with a wrought iron picture of a Ship's Captain that was mounted on the side of the building, attached to a swinging chain and below it was written, 'The Ship's End'. It was situated above the steps on the right of what was called the 'Little Beach'. The history of camaraderie, and foolery among the ship mates were apparent inside. The portraits and logbooks were vividly on display for all to see and read.

Ian was planning his little stunt on the beach, before the festivities began, ensuring that Frankie had a fresh set of clothes for the night ahead. He had conferred with the lads to dunk Frankie into the water giving him a bachelor's baptism before his big day.

They were all going to meet on the beach with a bottle of beer and then the festivities began. Dylan was right about the best man, a first-class prankster, let's hope Frankie takes it in good spirits. As Frankie turned to Ian he said,

'I wonder how the girls are doing, I bet it isn't going to be as good as this, you have excelled yourself mate, this Ship's End and the beach it's a beauty.

Ian answered back,

'It's just beginning mate, pace yourself'. They jump up and down and chanted, 'let's have a party', before making their way back into the pub.

It was going well in the girl's camp as everyone was arriving at the Castor Bar as Emily made her entrance, they all moved towards her,

They all shouted out,

'Wow! Don't you look like a princess'

'Let's get this party started! '

As the DJ started playing the music they all got up and danced as if they were ready for the Olympics. The energy from them didn't go unnoticed in the room as everyone's eyes were on the girls. Jacqueline and her sisters sat back and let the young ones take the stage, there was plenty of time to have dance later when the soul band arrived.

Sara looked tentatively at the lampshades and asked about the sparklers. Niamh danced her way to mam's table to get them up off their feet. Niamh explained to Sara at mid-night the sparklers will be lit as it will be Emily's last night of freedom...

Jacqueline pointed out it is a good job the wedding is days away, to give them time to recover from this night...

Niamh gave her mam a cheeky grin,

'Emily will be fine mam, we all will, it's time you were on the dance floor'.

Jacqueline was happy to just sit back,

'We are fine here watching you lot dancing; we are deep in our talking... about you lot'

Serena was enjoying herself on the dance floor and let herself go and felt better for it. There were so many people that turned up, Niamh wasn't sure who someone of them were, but it didn't matter it was going to be a great night!

The band were getting ready to come on, and everyone was up dancing, as Niamh grabbed her mam and sisters onto the dancefloor. The atmosphere in the bar just lit up when the band came on. They were so good, and the saxophone player just went for it as everyone was jumping up and down and swinging around.

The boys at this time were getting ready to take Frankie for a little swim in the water and some dunking and foolery was take place, as they all gathered on the beach, bantering away. Ian gave him a nod and up Frankie went into the air shouting,

'What the hell, you guys, supposed to be buddies!'

They splashed him up and down and they cheered,

'Frankie! Frankie! Come on lads let's give him the businesses, as they rolled him in the air and around and round and dunked him headfirst into the water!'

As they all splashed about, Ian turned to Frankie,

'You ok bud, enjoying herself'.

'Oh yeah bud, get you back!' as he pushed his best man in the water, they both sat in the water laughing their heads off.

That's your bachelor's baptism bud; we all have fresh clothes ready for your last night of freedom...

They all made their way to the Ship's End and got changed. Their night of music was the juke box as the band, 'Stackers'! booked for the night were delayed and may not make it!

The boys were not too bothered about that, as they were preparing for a card game later; the juke box was music enough for them.

Dylan sat by Colm, as they chatted for a moment about Colm's speech.

Frankie interrupted the conversation by saying,

'I hope you are going to be complimentary about your lovely sister and not make fun of her too much on our wedding day'.

Colm with his laid-back smile, sat back in his chair, and responded with,

'Me, I don't know what you mean our Emily is a vision of perfection, sometimes ... '

Frankie butted in,

'Oh! I don't like the sound of that Colm', as he laughed out loud, 'Make it a good one mate, I know you will'.

Meanwhile, the Hen party was in full swing, and the band was about to start and play. Sara made her move and got Jacqueline and Aileen on the floor, as they played the classics. The saxophone player was on good form; the place was now rocking...

As mid-night approached, the sparklers were lit, and Emily was taken to the stage, and she sang alongside the band as the sparklers sparkled away. The song, they were singing was,

'Everlasting love'. They all joined in, and everyone was jumping up and down as the whole room was lit up. It was sensational to see, as Emily sparkled as the bride to be. Niamh was so happy for her sister, and Jacqueline cried with joy for her daughter, she didn't know why she was crying the emotion just overtook her at that moment.

Serena was standing next to Jacqueline as they held hands. Jacqueline wanted to say something to Serena, but this was not the time to ask her how she was doing, she simply squeezed her hand and Serena acknowledged that and squeezed Jacqueline's hand in appreciation…

The boys were deep in their card game in the back room, and it was Colm who won the fiver. Dylan shouted up, 'Your round kiddo'.

They were merrily chanting out Frankie's name as they all huddled together and it was an eventful night despite the no show of the band, as they made their own amusement.

Colm got the drinks in, as they made their way to the juke box and began singing out, 'Be my baby', and 'I got you babe', as they merrily jumped up and down. Ian was trying to grab a mike from the bar to give his solo version of the songs, but the sound didn't come out! they all fell about in laughter at his silent portrayal of 'Be my baby'.

As the party came to an end, it was time for them to head home, the minibus had arrived and off they went to their beds. Frankie was the one who was suffering, he had gone too far with the whiskey drinking…

Emily was elated with her fabulous hen night and wasn't that worse for wear as she spent most of the time dancing rather than drinking. It was Niamh who had gone overboard! She didn't hold back! All her emotions had run wild this very night.

Niamh turned to Serena slurring her speech a little…

'You are so wonderful you know; you always look amazing'.

Serena who hadn't drank too much, she wasn't feeling herself but reciprocated and added,

'You are sloppy and drunk, but it is in a nice way'.

Jacqueline joined them and guided them to their minibus outside before giving her advice,

'You will have an awful headache Niamh in the morning I am sure', as she kissed her on the cheek.

Aileen and Sara commented on how brilliant Niamh had organised everything, they had not been to such a lavish hen party.

As the driver dropped everyone off, Niamh gave him a handsome tip, which he gratefully smiled and thanked her. He hadn't had a tip before; he was so taken back by it.

Emily, Niamh, and Jacqueline entered the cottage and Jacqueline asked if anyone wanted a drink of water or a cup of tea. Niamh gladly took a glass of water upstairs with her as the effect of drinking too much wine was taking its toll on her. Emily was the sensible one, and said to her mam,

'I wonder what time Colm will get in; I hope their night was as good as ours'.

Jacqueline hugged her daughter and responded,

'I am sure they have, I bet he will be home soon'.

Emily sat on her bed and Niamh was flat out, she started to quietly snore to Emily's annoyance...

She went back downstairs and sat in the kitchen with her mam, they talked of the wedding, and Declan not being there to give her away.

Jacqueline explained to Emily that it will be an emotional day without your father, but he will be there in spirit. I am sure he will be so proud of Colm giving you way.

As they sat and went through all the arrangements for the big day. They would start to organise pre-preparations the next day to save any mishaps... Emily felt so reassured by her mam's presence and she was comforted by her strength and fortitude.

They talked about the Beach House being renovated for them for the time being. Emily was so happy to have the Beach House as her first home, as she had such happy memories when she was young, as the Beach House was Jacqueline and Declan's first home...

Serena had provided the Flowers and Champagne for their first night together.

Aileen had supplied them with lovely new curtains and furnishings.

Sara had bought them a new bed.

Jacqueline had the Beach House signed over to them, it was theirs completely.

It was getting late, and they said their good nights...

Emily entered her bedroom, and Niamh was now sleeping soundly. As she put her head on her pillow, she fell into a deep sleep, thinking about her father and their happy times together at the Beach House...

Chapter 16

Niamh began to stir as her head spun around and around as she awoke early in the morning it was 6.30am. A sudden urge came upon her to be sick; she jumped out of bed and straight into the bathroom. The after-effects of her night of over-indulging especially on the sparkling wine. How she heaved her way through the morning and sipped on a glass of water, and groaned away…

'Oh! This is not good; I have never felt this bad before on No! as she spurted to the bathroom once more.

Emily turned over in the bed and shouted,

'It's your own fault, you really got carried away our Niamh, I have no sympathy whatsoever, suck it up sis'

Niamh came out of the bathroom, and stuck one finger up at her sister, which she had never done before.

Emily was stunned by her sister's gesture!

'I cannot believe you just did that our Niamh, my sister, behaving badly….

'Just drink lots of water today and have toast later, I will leave you to it'

Emily made her way downstairs to be greeted by her mam in the kitchen, they sat around the table discussing the night before. Jacqueline enquired about her daughter heaving upstairs and Emily assured her that she will be fine by the afternoon, she is overreacting our mam. Jacqueline looked a little concerned,

'Well, our Emily, it is just as well we have few days of recovery before the wedding, I hope your Frankie is, ok? I have not heard from Colm; he must have stayed at Frankie's as he is not in his bed…'

Jacqueline entered the bedroom and took one look at Niamh and gave her a wry smile,

'I am not surprised you look awful; you certainly went full throttle with the wine drinking last night dear girl. I would suggest you keep to water today; I will bring a jug up to you and a glass, no point in you coming downstairs, stay close to the bathroom'.

Niamh mumbled away,

'Aww thanks mam', as she lifted her head up from the toilet.

Emily made her way downstairs to telephone Frankie to see how he was faring this morning, she was hoping he wasn't in such as state as her sister.

The telephone rang and rang out and just as she was about to put the receiver down, Colm answered the telephone.

'Hi, our Em, how are you doing, how is everyone, as he tried to divert the conversation from Frankie.

Frankie at this time was sprawled across his bed with his head hanging over the side, with a bucket by him in readiness for those splurges of being sick... It was not a pretty sight; he was feeling the full-on effects of his stag night. It was the latter part of the night that swung it, as he couldn't remember drinking the last shots of whiskey.

Emily was getting impatient with Colm and demanded to know where Frankie was as she wanted to speak to him. Colm was trying to explain to Emily that he had gone for a walk to clear his head, which of course was a bare-faced lie, but he wasn't going to explain the situation as he didn't want his sister to get het up as he knew she would!

The conversation was left at that point, as Colm resolved the situation by telling Emily that Frankie would call her later that day. As Colm put the telephone down, he went into Frankie's bedroom to tell him to get his act together and have a cold bath!

Frankie looked up at Colm,

'A cold bath! Seriously! bud, really!

Colm pulled him up,

'I am deadly serious, I have just told your future wife a whopping lie, so get it together! You need to speak to her this afternoon; I promised you would'

Frankie gave out a full-blown groan and shouted out!

'I think I am dying! What the hell happened last night, I remember the dunking in the sea, but after that I cannot remember much'

Colm sat by Frankie's side on the bed and began telling him the whole story of the latter part of the night.

Well, after we give you a good dunking and downed a few beers, we headed into the pub. Ian the best man arranged with Joe the pub landlord to have the back room for our card game, and a lock- in was set up for after hours. That my friend was when you were in full swing lad, you insisted on downing the shots, yes, you got really carried away mate, seriously. At one point I told Ian that was enough, he was as bad as you mate.

We left the pub at 2am and Joe and I bundled you into a taxi, myself being the caretaker of you. Ian was not fit to take care of you, he was met with an angry girlfriend who was not too pleased, and she took him home. Ian apparently called her up in the pub in a drunken stupor, more fool him; he will get in the neck that's for sure when he wakes up today. Jenny will throttle him! His hangover will last for days before Jenny is finished with him! They both laughed out loud, poor Ian...

The telephone rang out and it was Dylan, who called to see how Frankie was as he was a little concerned about him. Colm replied by saying,

'He looks like a drowned rat'

Dylan gave a sarcastic reply to that,

'How ironic given that he was virtually drowned last night laughing out loud, is he ok though?

Colm turned to look at Frankie and pointed to the bathroom, nudging him to go and get that cold bath! He put the receiver to his ear and said to Dylan,

'He is not too bad, he is making out he is dying, he is having a cold bath under my instructions, he needs it to wake him up. I told Emily a big lie, he was out walking, he must call her this afternoon'

Dylan could hear Serena in the background, she seemingly was making a rather gagging sound, Dylan was diverted and told Colm he was ringing off and would catch up later.

Serena at this time was kneeling, with the toilet seat up as Dylan entered the bathroom,

'Oh love, not you too, did you have too much to drink?'

As Serena got up and wiped her mouth and interposed,

'I didn't drink that much love at all, I have felt a bit queasy these last few days.

They both stared into each other's eyes and spoke at the same time.

'Are we pregnant do you think'

Serena checked her diary and looked for her last period and gave Dylan a startled look and spoke.

'Oh, my I hadn't realised it's been two months! I have been so wrapped up with work, it hadn't occurred to me. I thought I had eaten something that had disagreed with me…

'Let's not get carried away love, let's just wait and see, I will make an appointment with the Doctor tomorrow, and see what he has to say'.

They both sat quietly for some time not sure whether to be elated or to be concerned, could they handle these emotions, it had only been a few months since the miscarriage. Serena wasn't sure how she felt at this time, and Dylan was so confused, he decided to go for a run and give Serena a little space.

He started his run from the lighthouse, the sultry spray layered itself alongside the Lighthouse, as Dylan looked up, he couldn't help but notice how illuminating the lighthouse looked, it was if the spray had enlightened the whole structure of it.

He then sat down on the wooden bench, and watched the waves slither in and out with that glorious spray surrounding the lighthouse, as it touched his feet, he began to feel very emotional and his thoughts turned to his brother Declan and how he wished so much he could sit and talk to him, for he needed his voice at this time.

His head fell into his knees and as he looked up Father Donnelly appeared and greeted him as he tilted his biretta,

'Good morning, Dylan, what a beautiful morning it is; that beautiful shining spray surrounding the sea certainly gives us food for thought, the wonders of nature don't you think?'

Dylan looked up with a surprised look on this face as he couldn't speak for a moment, but he knew what Father Donnelly meant, for it was spray on the lighthouse that had affected him so profoundly, he didn't know why it had affected him so?

Father Donnelly sat by his side he could always tell when there was something wrong, he had seen that vulnerable look on many faces in his lifetime, but he was not going to pry unless Dylan wanted to offer his thoughts to him.

Well Father, I feel like I am at a crossroads, something happened this morning that triggered elation and anxiety at this time. It is rather confusing, as it may turn out to be a false alarm and the elation will have flitted away, but I don't want the elation to flitter away, and at the same time the anxiety of the situation seems to flood my thoughts of painful times to come as they did in the past.

Father Donnelly had an incline of what Dylan's was trying to say and gave out a candid reply,

'The way I see it lad, life wouldn't be life without elation and anxiety in it, the two go together like peas in a pod; the secret is to manage both with courage, bravery, and of course a good sense of humour helps in all cases. Do not let your heart be troubled or afraid, trust yourself and your strong instincts. You can do this lad, you are as strong as your brother, you just don't know it yet'.

Dylan looked into Father Donnelly's eyes and shook his hand and thanked him for his kind words of wisdom.

Father Donnelly once again tipped is biretta and wished Dylan a good day as he whistled by the lighthouse and onto the beach road for this constitutional walk, how he loved his walks. Everyone would wish him good morning as he passed by.

Dylan at this time felt a sense of calmness and continued his run with vigour and energy, he ran with such conviction. As he made his way back home, he saw a note on the telephone table. Serena had gone to Jacquelines, and she would be back in a few hours. He smiled at himself in the mirror.

'Where else would she go but Jacqueline's said he'

He went off to have a shower, feeling so completely happy in himself, he would tackle that garden fence before Serena came home.

Serena had arrived at Jacquelines', and she had already set the table with tea and biscuits. They both sat down, and Jacqueline remarked on how Serena looked very pale this morning. As they made their way to the kitchen Serena turned to Jacqueline,

'I have been queasy these past weeks, and thought it was indigestion, I am not sure now'

Jacqueline sat back in the chair and began by saying,

'Let's take a step at a time, firstly, get into see your GP as soon as possible, see if he can get you in tomorrow morning'

It was a sleepless night for Serena, but instead of calling the GP she arrived at 8.45am in readiness for 9.00am when the doors opened. She sat tentatively watching the clock, 9.00am came and the receptionist opened the doors.

She was told that there had been a cancellation for the 9.15am slot and she was so relieved to hear that as she sat tapping her feet up and down until her ankles ached.

Finally! Her name was called to see Dr Caitlin. Serena had brought a specimen of her early morning urine in readiness, and Dr Caitlin took it to be analysed which would take a few days, but he asked Serena to get undressed whilst he examined her.

As Serena got dressed and sat in the seat opposite Dr Caitlin, he began by saying that he was almost certain she was pregnant six weeks pregnant was his diagnosis. He was confident the urine test would verify this.

Serena sat in a motionless state and Dr Caitlin repeated himself and asked if she was alright. Serena looked into his eyes, and said,

'I am ecstatic Dr Caitlin, truly I am'

They both smiled at each other and wished each other a good day. Serena would call the surgery.

She walked towards her car, as if she was dancing on air, she felt so light. She must call Dylan he will be at work by now, and then her parents, and call at Jacquelines.

The roads were busy, and she was getting impatient to get home, but took her time, she didn't want anything happening at this stage, not like last time, no more adventurous rides or stunts with this pregnancy.

Eventually she arrived home and rushed to the telephone it was sometime before they located Dylan at the shipyard, he was stunned by the call and couldn't wait to get home later to share the joy with Serena.

All day he had a smile on his face and his crew were fascinated by his eager smiling and whistling for they hadn't seen such a performance from Dylan, as he had been so sombre these past months. The Crew were so uplifted as the atmosphere in the cabin was swarming with good cheer...

Serena would call round to see her parents later that day, as she wanted to get to Jacqueline's first to share her good news. Jacqueline had been such a good support for Serena in the past.

They decided to walk along the promenade as the sun was coming out and it would be nice to just saunter and take in the delights of the beautiful coastline; the sandy beach glistened like gold. They would stop at Manchello's for an iced tea.

Serena remarked on the beautiful view, the seating area was adjacent to the lifeguards and the surfers, they were already out on the water.

The conversation then turned to the wedding as there is two days to go and Serena would have had her test back hopefully before the wedding.

As they both looked at each other and said simultaneously,

'It will be a day of love, happiness and joy for all of us....

Chapter 17

Serena awoke on this sunny spring morning as she contemplated that call to her doctor's surgery. Today was the day where she would finally know the outcome of whether she was truly pregnant? Her feelings of hope and despair came upon her.

'Why oh! why am I feeling so apprehensive, Dr Caitlin said he was 99% sure, oh Why am I feeling like this? Said she.

As she put her dressing gown and made her way to the dressing table and looked at herself through the dresser mirror which was attached to the dressing table. Serena sat in a trance for some time, until she heard a mumbled voice in the background, it was Dylan calling her.

'Serena my love, you are going to be late for work, it is 8.15am, where are you at girl, I am off to work catch you later love as he shouted upstairs.

She then jumped up and went racing into the bathroom and was dressed and made up by 8.45am. She then made her way to the telephone and eventually got through to Dr Caitlin, he replied by congratulating Serena on her pregnancy, and he would like to see her in 6 weeks for her first check up and he would send in a referral to the maternity department at Tyneside Hospital to take care of her from then on.

As she put the telephone down, she began to cry incessantly and quickly dried her eyes as she was going to be late for work. It was a good job her secretary had booked the first client in for 10.00am as per instructions.

'Phew I should make it in time,' said she.

It was day of events all round, as the Gibson household were in a frenzy, they were making sure everything was in place for the wedding day.

Frankie was still feeling that dull ache in his head, but he was determined to get it together and vowed never to be in that state again.

Niamh was on light food and water until after the wedding, and vowed she would toast the bride and groom with sparkling water... As for Emily she was a busy bee; she had already arrived at the venue to make quite sure everything was in place. She then paid a visit to Father Donnelly to check on the flowers at the church as she was a stickler for detail.

Father Donnelly greeted her with his usual jovial self, and they sat down to wait for Frankie who was due at the church to go through the last-minute arrangements, he was late as usual. A loud sound appeared accompanied with a clatter, as Frankie pushed his way through the heavy Tudor style doors that were made of solid oak.

As he gasped for his breath, Father Donnelly got up to greet him.

'Well young man you made it, how are you this fine morning,' said he

Frankie, gulped and then spurted out in a nervous tone,

'I am faring well, Father, thank you', as he gave an apologetic look to Emily who was rolling her eyes at this point.

Father Donnelly suggested they make their way to the presbytery where is housekeeper would make them a cup of tea or coffee. He felt it would be best to conduct matters informally as he noticed how nervous Frankie was looking, and he was right. Frankie at this time gave out a small sigh of relief.

The Father made the whole experience so inviting with his light-hearted approach, Frankie and Emily left the church so relaxed and at ease at they walked to the car park hand in hand.

As Frankie turned to Emily with a sincere look, he went on to say,

'I am such a lucky man, Emily Gibson, I will never let you down, I promise'

Emily kissed him with such passion and replied with a loving gesture,

'I wouldn't expect anything else, for I too, would never have imagined I would be meet someone as wonderful as you Frankie Gallagher'.

Meanwhile, Jacqueline was busy cleaning the whole cottage, it was her way of not dwelling on Declan not being there for his first daughter being married. She went at her chores with such vigour, it was bringing out her strength of character to try and move on, but at this time the anger would show its ugly face, as she must have polished that dining room table over and over, it was gleaming!

Colm had left his mother to it, as he was going to enjoy his day off work, and meet up with Bernadette at the beach, as they were going to sketch out the prominent Lighthouse and attaching shoreline, it was a day for it, as the sun shone out so much. The sand seemed to reflect the heat of the moment as it looks like it was changing colour to a sultry cream image.

It was trying time though for Niamh as she was still feeling a little fragile, her mission for the day was to sit outside and hit the books as she had a lot to catch up, as her teaching course was well into the third semester and there was still so much to do.

As the hours past, she tried to invite her mam to join her, in the hope that she could turn her mam's thoughts to literature and how she was getting on with her course.

It took a while before Jacqueline gave in and joined her daughter, it turned out to be more rewarding that she thought, as Jacqueline began to get animated about her course and where she was going in the future. It was like she was living in a different world, and she liked it a lot.

They spent so many hours outside in the sun, they hadn't noticed how sun burned they were getting, as they laughed at this each other, April! And sunburned, whatever next!

Jacqueline went in to grab the sun blockers and brought some lemonade out, and glanced over at the kitchen clock,

'We better pack up pet it is getting near teatime, and we should prepare for the pre wedding dinner my pet, let's make it a great one,' said she.

As Niamh turned her head towards her mam,

'We should have a picnic style send-off saying it's so sunny and bright, we can do hot beef and chicken sandwiches mam, and everyone can just tuck in to what they fancy. Let's invite everyone mam, Dylan, Serena, and her parents, and my aunts and uncles, let's just have a great party mam', said she.

It was settled and everyone arrived at 6pm and they had a great get together, it was low key where the alcohol was concerned as everyone wanted to be sharp and alert on the big day, which was now beckoning.

Frankie was having a quiet time with his family, being the only surviving son, it was a quiet concern. His brother John had drowned at the age of ten years. It had embarked on a school trip and ventured out on his own without permission.

The class was over heavy being twenty-seven pupils and it was tragic accident at the lake side where they were on a geography field trip.

No one had noticed at the time that John had slipped away, he had been attracted by the wildlife in the water and as he bent over to take a closer look in slipped on the edge of the slimy leafy ledge and went headfirst. He was a not a great swimmer and by the time they had noticed he was gone it was too late to revive him.

The household was in good spirits for the sake of Frankie's big day. Gerald and Agnes made a night of it with Frankie. His mam made his favourite steak and kidney pie and Frankie, and his father played a game of dominos, before he set off to Ian's place as he was staying with his best man for the night.

It was a melancholy night as all of them glanced at John's portrait on the sideboard, that reminder of how vibrant and full of energy he was. They all decided that the cherished memories will be that of laughter and joy.

It was time for Frankie to make his way to Ian's. He was having one pint! Ian joked and said,

'Well mate, we cannot have a repeat of your stag night, that's for sure', he laughed out loud at the thought of it'.

It turned out to be a quiet night in watching the television, it was good job there was a sports programme on, they were both elated and sat back and enjoyed their bottle of beer.

The nightfall came upon them, and it was now 6am and Frankie and Ian were up and ready. Ian pointed out that they didn't need to be at the barbers until 9.30am,

'Plenty of time mate, let's chill,'

Frankie lay back on the sofa in his boxer shorts and couldn't believe this day had arrived, he was going to get married, and he was going to be in that beautiful cottage by the sea, thanks to Jacquline and the late Declan. He pinched himself to make sure it was real…

Emily too was up with the lark organising everyone hours beforehand. Her mam got her to slow down, as she reminded her that her asthma was under control, but if she carried on like this, she would bring an attack on. She gave her mam an approving look and tentatively listened to her mam for once as they sat at the kitchen table and sipped their tea.

'That's better our Emily, it makes sense, said Jacqueline.

Time seemed to get on very quickly and it was now 9.am it was time.

'Let's make tracks our Emily, the Hairdresser will be waiting for us' said Jacqueline.

They made their way to Michelle's Hair Salon, which was situated on the corner of promenade.

Emily decided she would have her hair up in a curly bun with two ringlets that would drop down by the side of her face. Her sister Niamh went over to her and asked if she would mind if she could have her hair down in flowing curls, as she liked it best. Emily put her arm around her dear sister and said,

'You can have your hair anyway you like sis, you always look beautiful, for you are the looker of the family'

Niamh shook her head and disagreed,

'You are more beautiful inside and out; Dad would always say that I know,' said she.

They both hug each other tightly and agreed we must get on, as time was the essence.

Jacqueline joined in,

'My hair is so easy my bob style will be done in a jiffy' as she smiled at her two wonderful daughters. It was a simple and easy choice for the hairdresser. The youngest stylist took care of Jacqueline as Michelle supervised whilst doing Emily's hair.

Afterwards, everyone made their way back to Jacqueline's to get ready, Colm was already suited and booted ready for Emily, he was eager.

Jacqueline complimented her son on how grown up and dapper he looked this very day. Colm bowed to his mam with a rather majestic look on his face... as he raised one eyebrow.

'Thank you, dear mother, I am most obliged' as he swung is left arm outwards and bowed most effectively.

Jacqueline's grin on her face said it all,

'At ease young man straighten yourself up now,' said she.

Louisa helped Emily with her dress and veil, and as she put the tiara onto her head, she gleamed with love for her dearest friend and said,

'Wow' best friend, you look like a movie star my lass'

Emily turned to her friend and ushered her in the corner to get ready. They sat for a moment and the door opened and in popped Niamh and her mam.

Jacqeline was filled with emotion,

'I am not going to hug you pet, as I don't want to ruffle you, just want to say how amazing you look pet'

They all gathered in the living room and Emily turned to her bridesmaids and gave them all a bracelet, inscription read, 'bridesmaid', which complimented their beautiful lemon and daisy style dresses.

She went over to her mam and gave her a silver compact with an inscription of mother of the bride, Jacqueline was so moved by this, but she wasn't going to let her emotions run away with her, not just yet anyway.

They were already for the wedding cars to arrive, as Frankie and Ian and guests were all standing by at the church, listening to Father Donnelly's jovial jokes, his Irish tone resonated throughout the congregation. The Church was lit up with divine joy and laughter on this special day.

Colm got of the wedding car as it pulled up at the church and opened the door in a gentleman like manner to escort Emily to the entrance of the church.

'Our Colm I am so proud of you, you are my rock today, you truly are,' said she

Colm gulped a breath and stood tall, as he was taking his father's place and he was going to act as his father taught him, with dignity and pride.

The choir stood by as the soprano Beverly was to sing Ave Maria with a small group of musicians, a guitarist, a violinist and a pianist.

Frankie began to fill up as he caught his first glimpse of his bride to be, he too would stand tall and keep his emotions in check.

The lengthy service was over, and they were all outside for the photographers, the sun was out once again, and everyone was talking over one another.

Frankie's mam and dad were so impressed with such a beautiful service as they had never been to a Catholic service before. They were so happy for their son but felt that sense of loss once more as they would have to carry on without any of their sons in the house from now on. It was Gerald who turned to Agnes and said,

'We will be alright pet, he hasn't moved away, we will still see him from time to time, let's enjoy yourselves today pet'

Agnes nodded emotionally back to her husband. Frankie and Emily made their way over to them and invited them to tea once they got settled. Agnes was taken back by this and didn't hold back.

'You two need your own time together for a bit, we can call you in a few weeks, how's that sound'

Frankie gave his mam a tight squeeze and whispered,

'Thank you, mam, love you'

Agnes looked on at Emily who had such a kind and generous heart, and at that moment she realised she was inheriting a beautiful daughter in law, it felt that she had a daughter now in her family. A sense of warm and belonging came over her.

All the photographs were now taken, and all parties made their way to the Pavilion, Father Donnelly thanked Frankie and Emily for their invite, but he pointed out that his job was done and they just needed to enjoy themselves. He thanked them for their generous donation to the church.

The Pavilion was magnificently presented just as Emily had ordered. Mr Kitson the manager gave her nodding approval as he glanced at the pebbled beach stone figurines on each table, they certainly did make the most exquisite centre piece on each table that glistened with a powerful flow of perfection that resonated around the room, for everything look so perfect.

The speeches began, Colm was well controlled he pointed out to Frankie that he was getting a top prize with Emily, but watch out for her prickly temper, she may wash you out with a certain look, Frankie acknowledged that as he had first-hand experience, especially after the stag night, he won't forget that look…

It was the best man to stand up, and Ian didn't hold back, he started with the good side and then went on to say that Frankie can be a bit of prankster himself, for he is well known for sending you stuff through mail that is so ridiculous for words, he once delivered to my house a frog, yes, as I opened it, the frog repeatedly said,

'Ribbit, ribbit, ribbit, ribbit'

I think he was trying to tell me something, like, 'button it in future'

So, watch out Emily for what the postman might bring to you one day'

The whole room resonated with laughter at this point

It was now time for the meal to be served. The roast beef just melted in your mouth, with glorious tastes of homemade farm food. The presentation of the food was met with compliments galore from everyone.

As they took to the dancefloor for the first dance, as the band sang, 'Can't take my eyes you' as they candidly waltzed in their fashion around the dance floor, laughing, as Franking stood on Emily's foot.

Serena and Dylan and everyone took the dancefloor, gleaming with joy and love for their future ahead.

Colm sat with his mam, his mam put her arm around her son and quietly spoke,

'Your Dad would have been too,'

Colm turned to his mam,

'I think he was here today mam, I felt his presence, I really did,'

Niamh approached them and got them both to step onto the dance floor as they all danced together.

The night was coming to an end, and Frankie and Emily made their way to the bride and groom suite on the top floor of the Pavilion.

As the door shut Frankie opened it and put a 'Do not disturb' sign.... Outside the door... ...

Chapter 18

The months drifted by and on this restful Monday morning, the sunrise spread itself all over the beautiful coastline. A sparkle of light transformed Sandhaven Beach as it glittered like gold.

A warm glow came over Jacqueline as she opened her curtains and looked out at the harmonious view, the stillness of a glowing light resonating over a dusky sky, as the clouds mingled and lay themselves bare. It was moment to savour and never let go. She was feeling that poetic string of nature, and its picturesqueness came flooding through.

She put on her dressing gown and hurried outside to take in the breathtaking view, as she scribbled a short poem;

A Sky of Gold
A story to be told
A sunrise so bright
So shiny and upright
A quiver of calm
A divine psalm.
A harmony so sweet
A sacred place to retreat

Jacqueline was consumed with a calming stance, as she watched the waves smoothly glide in and out in what seemed a limitless movement. She sat motionless as she watched the beauty of the waves fold around the frothy like substance. It was Colm who shouted as he opened the back door; it made Jacqueline jump! as she heard his loud voice as he opened the back door.

'Mam what are you doing out here! it's not even 6 am mam, I just came down for a drink of water and saw the backdoor open, I thought we had burglars!' said he

Jacqueline turned her head around to Colm,

'Oh, Son, the sunrise and the breathtaking view, I could not resist it'.

Colm shook his head,

'Oh, mam, you and your poems and writings, you are a one off, I swear you are, as he smiled back his mam; I am going back to bed, and you should too mam'.

Jacqueline was so wide awake as she sat at the bottom of the garden, her thoughts turned to the week ahead. She was so looking forward to attending University…She had gotten rid of her fears of further education. The Creative Writing course at college had given her that boost of confidence she so dearly needed…

She was excited about the morning lecture in the big hall, 'Lyon's Hall'. Professor Macpherson was giving the lecture on post-modern literature. It sounded so appealing as Jacqueline hadn't read any novels of this era.

As she sat and looked out at the ocean she was suddenly overwhelmed with her newfound life as a mature student.

'Will I get through this, will I achieve something out of this, I have to, it was my dream as a teenager', said she.

She quickly gathered her thoughts and made her way back into the cottage, it was time to get the day started properly. Niamh was already up and dressed to take her mam to the university, as she too was ready for her morning lectures.

They both had a quick breakfast, cereal and a cup of tea before heading off for the day. As Niamh got into the car she turned to her mam,

'Are you ready for this mam, it's been quite a weekend, hasn't it?

I am so looking forward to getting on with the course now, I so want to get into teaching now and earning some money, as you and dad have been so generous with me, I want to pay you back mam'

Jacqueline was taken back by such a grand gesture and quickly replied,

'We didn't do it so we could be compensated for wanting our talented daughter to achieve her goals. Niamh sweetheart, there is no need to think about pay back of any sorts, you just concentrate on your studies and getting where you must be. Your dad and I just wished for your happiness and success, and we have it, that was our prize nothing more'

Niamh drove quietly for the next few miles, but she wasn't satisfied with her mam's response, she would make it up to her later in her life, she was determined to do that. The conversation was diverted by Niamh as she was interested in her mam's plans now, Jacqueline had achieved her 'O' levels in English and Creative Writing, but she wasn't getting anything positive from her Mam.

Jacqueline went onto say she was enjoying her new direction in life, and she hadn't thought that far ahead, and she would give it more thought towards the end of her diploma, which wouldn't be for another 12 months.

They had arrived at the campus and hugged each other and went their separate ways. Jacqueline went through the double doors on the west wing of the campus as that was where the lecture was taking place. As she entered the room, she was surprised to see that it was almost full, everyone had come in early?

She slowly made her way down the centre of the lecture room to see if she could spot either Jillian or Louise, as she stepped halfway down the hall, she heard a voice saying,

'Jacqueline, here, there is a room here for you to sit'.

It was Jillian her old friend, as she got up to make room for Jacqueline.

Jacqueline was happy to see her, as it was nice feeling to have a familiar face in the lecture room, it made it less daunting.

They both sat and chatted about the lecture it was an interesting one. 'Emancipation of Women and pursuit to freedom, and what affect it had on society and how it influenced both male and female writers of that time'.

As Professor Macpherson took to the floor, Jacqueline froze for a moment, all her inner self went numb at his appearance. He walked liked Declan, and he looked like Declan. She felt like she was seeing ghost! It was most unsettling, as she tried to take in the volume of content about the writers of that time. She could hardly take any of it in, it was just as well that Jillian had written everything down and she would ask her if she could compare notes, to what little note Jacqueline had achieved at this point.

She gathered herself quickly and began writing furiously about how women began to liberate themselves and become their own person in a male domineering world.

Professor Macpherson certainly knew how to captivate his audience with such panache, as each student was writing on their note pads with such energy. He shouted out to everyone,

'Put your pens, pencils down everyone as it is time for questions and answers, you, that is to say, everyone here has the chance to lecture me and ask me any questions you like on the subject of this literature course'

The room was so silent you could hear a pin drop. There were fluttering's and flustering's amongst all the students who looked so anxious at the Professor's request to ask a question. Jacqueline turned her head to look at others and noticed no one had put their hand up to go first. She mustered up enough courage and stood up and said,

'I have a question; do you believe that emancipation of women's rights at the time period you stipulated would ever come to fruition as it seems a long way off from a male domineering world'

Professor Macpherson was spellbound! he couldn't take his eyes off Jacqueline! He gave out a nervous cough and answered in his eloquent style,

'It was new era a new movement that was shifting and it was alarming to the male species at the time. The suffragettes were a prime example of how the world was changing and yes, it was a slow process, but in retrospect it was a great moment for all women to achieve at least some change in social conditioning, so in essence it was making progress'

Jacqueline sat down, her stomach was churning away, her heartbeat was beating too fast for her liking. Jillian looked across at Jacqueline,

'Oh, Jacqueline are you ok? You looked so flushed?' said she.

Jillian held her hand, as she noticed how Jacqueline had reacted to Professor Macpherson when he first entered the lecture hall. She had seen a photograph of Declan on their get together of reminiscing the past. She too could not help but notice the canny resemblance of the professor and Declan.

The lecture was over, and the room began to empty, the professor made a bee line towards Jacqueline as she looked up and quivered, he thanked her for her excellent question and hoped she would enjoy his course. She nervously said she would and was looking forward to learning more about the period writers and their films, as the second part of the course was novel to screen which excited Jacqueline a lot.

She said her goodbyes to the professor; her whole day was fixed around that moment of meeting him. She couldn't get him out of her mind or was it she couldn't stop thinking of Delcan, she was confused as her thoughts were so conflicting. The day ended with her having such a tense headache as she took to the cupboard at home and reached for the aspirin, she never liked to take tablets, but she needed them tonight.

Niamh entered the kitchen and looked a little concerned about her mam,

'Mam, you have been acting a little strange since the drive back home, what is going on mam?'

Jacqueline, put her glass down on the table she looked rather pale as she sat down and began telling Niamh of how shocked she looked when meeting the professor for the first time and how it struck her like a bolt of lightning as if she was seeing Declan again!

Niamh stuttered with amazement for a moment and said,

'Oh, I must get a look at this man, see for myself, when is your next lecture with him?'

'It's on Wednesday at 9am' Niamh replied.

'I have not got a lesson until eleven on that day right I am coming into the hall with you'

Colm was home, awaiting his tea, nothing was prepared, he looked stunned to see them sitting there with no smell of any kind of food.

'Is it chippy night mam? I can't smell any food. It is 6 o'clock mam, teatime, food time...'

Jacqueline apologised to her son and gave him few pounds to get his favourite supper from the local chippy, she wasn't hungry, but Colm brought back extra portions. He as starving! They all ate up, apart from Jacqueline who hardly touched her food.

Colm was intrigued and tried to pry an explanation from his mam, but she was reluctant to talk about her day and just said it had been a trying day. He then turned to Niamh and nodded his head sideways to get a reaction from Niamh as he lowered his voice,

'What is going on our Niamh, mam looks a little ill, what happened today'

Niamh took Colm into the living room and shut the door and sat Colm down and told him the whole story, he too wouldn't mind having a look at the professor. He was keen on getting to the university at some stage to see for himself, but wouldn't be able to get there on Wednesday, and made it is mission to get there on another day. He asked to Niamh to keep him informed of any further developments on this mysterious look alike.

'My dad having a lookalike, what about that then man!'

Jacqueline took to her room and got out all the photographs of Declan, it all came flooding back the memories, the devastation, she couldn't get over the professor it was if Declan had been reincarnated! Was it a lovely feeling as her heart glowed with love once again, she felt so uneasy as she slept that night dreaming of them both, she couldn't wait until Wednesday as she counted off the hours on the Tuesday.

Wednesday morning had arrived, and Jacqueline was up at 6am bathed and getting out her best shirt and blouse, she was making the most of her figure and didn't wear much make up. She didn't need a lot of make up as her skin was impeccable, all that sea air and long walks kept her skin in good condition over the years.

She looked in the mirror at herself before questioning herself,

'What am I doing, who am I, who is this lady, she doesn't look like me anymore, who has taken over me'.

She smiled at herself and loved this feeling of excitement she had not felt like this for such a long time, it was like she was going to meet Declan her Declan.

Niamh was up now,

'Mam, crikey you are ready and dressed, look at you, you look so young mam! Wow! A total transformation, I would what has brought about such a transformation?' As she winked at her mam.

Time went by and they were ready to get into the car and off to the lecture hall. Niamh seemed as excited as her mam to see this mysterious look alike that has caused so much chaos! They entered the lecture hall and Niamh commented on how full it was,

'Mam is it this full all the time, wow!

When I go to my lectures on teaching, they are half full, he must be good eh?'

Professor Macpherson entered the room and Niamh's colour from her rosy cheeks seem to drain away, she was gobsmacked at what a resemblance, his walk, his eyes, his build. The only difference she could differentiate was his posh accent. Oh my God! How could this be, it was like she was seeing her father back in the room. She soon realised he had differences when he spoke with such panache, and he was so charismatic and even seem to flirt with the young ladies in the room.

Jacqueline, however, seem to be besotted with him. Niamh noticed he looked at her mam quite a lot all through the lecture, she seemed to be disturbed by that. She was worried about her mam and the influence he may have over her; she felt it wasn't healthy...

After the lecture, the professor seemed to hurry towards Jacqueline to get her views on the lecture. Niamh had a chance to have a good look at this man, and she was suspicious of his actions towards her mam. She knew he was nothing like her real dad, as she shook his hand.

There was something about him that didn't sit right with Niamh, and she was going to find out more about this man. He didn't wear a wedding ring, but there was a mark around the third finger, left hand and it seemed to her that a ring had been permanently planted there, just removed for a time... Oh yes, she was going to pursue this man incognito of course, as he is hiding something...

Chapter 19

Serena and Dylan arrived at the maternity outpatient's department it was to be their first check up since they received their happy news of twins to arrive in early new year…

Dylan looked to Serena with such concern as he held her hand; he was worried as she was having frequent dizzy spells, and her ankles began to swell rapidly.

The nurse arrived and called them in to see Dr Hamilton, he took her blood pressure and was alarmed to see it was quite high. He quickly examined her, and as she sat up, he began to inform her that she would need either to be admitted for rest or she could be rested at home if she didn't exert herself in any way.

Serena turned to Dylan with a tearful look on her face. Dr Hamilton assured them both that the babies heart beats were fine, but the blood pressure was a concern so no stress or strain. He would see her again in 4 weeks' time to see how she is doing.

As they both left the hospital Dylan comforted Serena and helped her into the car. He began saying that he thought it would be a good idea if his mother-in-law came to stay for a while to keep her company whilst he was at work.

Serena was still in shock and couldn't think of anything now, as she was so worried about her babies, it was hitting her harder than she thought. She couldn't lose these babies oh no! not again! She shouted out!

'Dylan! I am not going back to work, I am not losing my babies, I am going to stay home, please! say that's ok, I know it would be financial suicide at the minute, but I don't want to lose my babies!'

He stopped the car and put his hands around Serena's face, and made his loving gesture,

'I love you and I love our babies, money doesn't come into my love, you stay at home, and I am pleased you said that as I would have said it '

Serena gave out uncontrollable tears of joy, they both shed a tear and made their way home. Dylan would telephone Charlotte, and he would call on Jacqueline after work to see if she had any time to spend with Serena.

Charlotte arrived that very afternoon and was happy to support her daughter.

'I don't mind pet doing the day shift, I charge £5 an hour' as she winked at her Serena.

'I will need some books mum, some puzzles, or something to keep me occupied. I wonder if you would kindly go to the library and find me some conspiracy novels, also, some detective stories to keep me amused'.

A smile on face, Charlotte was out the door and back within the hour with a bundle of goodies for Serena to read.

'These should keep you busy for a week or two I should think'

It was almost coming up to teatime and Dylan was on the road towards Jacquelines. As he pulled up, Niamh's car was just parking with Jacqueline in the passenger seat. He waved to them as he got out of the car.

'Uncle Dylan, so lovely to see you, it seems ages since we have seen you' said Niamh,

Dylan put his arms around Niamh,

'How's it going my niece, you are looking good girl'

As he turned his head towards Jacqueline.

'Are you ok there our Jacqueline' with a puzzled look on his face

'Let's get in shall we and get the kettle on' as Jacqueline put the key in the door.

They all made their way to the kitchen and Niamh began the conversation about the Professor. As Dylan slumped back in his chair, he was amazed at what he was hearing. His response was,

'Our Declan, a lookalike how extraordinary, I must meet this guy sometime'

'You might just be in luck as he seems to be smitten with our mam, giving her loads attention'.

'Oh really, what is this then'

Jacqeline blushed, as she interrupted the conversation,

'She is exaggerating, he pays a lot of attention to lots of students'

Niamh shook her head towards Dylan, suggesting that was not true at all.

The subject changed for a moment and Dylan explained about Serena and her condition and Jacqueline was concerned but she would not be able to find any time to see her, but she would call her tonight.

Jacqueline was so consumed with her thoughts and feelings of the mysterious professor. She hadn't divulged the secret conversation they had that day whereby they would both meet tomorrow for a one-to-one consultation with coffee and biscuits. Jacquelines heart started to beat faster… She couldn't think of anyone or anything else…

Niamh saw Dylan to the door; and had a private word with him outside as she relayed her fears and worries about the professor.

Dylan seemed a little unconcerned about what he was told, and he advised Niamh to give him the benefit of the doubt as he thought Jacqueline was glowing and hadn't seen her looking so well in herself since Declan's death.

Niamh said her goodbyes and she too would call in to see Serena at the weekend. As she went back into the house, she decided to call Sara and Aileen for their input on the situation. Sara suggested they all meet up on Thursday night for further discussions on the subject…

Jacqueline took to her bedroom early; she was wanting to be alone with her thoughts and feelings. Niamh would see to herself for tea as Colm was out at Bernadettes as they were having a meal out.

Oh! So glad our Colm is making a permanent move towards Bernadette now, it's about time!' said she.

It was getting dark, and moonlight was shining its happy face over the sea and sand, as Jacqueline looked out of her bedroom she muttered,

'The moon, the wishing well of dreams, that ripple and drizzle into a love-like stream…

She was still engulfed with the mirror image of Declan; it was if she was making her beloved immortal with her feelings towards the professor…

Niamh was looking forward to seeing her aunts to set out plans to find out about the professor's personal life. She had heard rumours that the professor is married but they have a turbulent relationship! She must pursue more information in her mind and hoped her aunts would assist her.

Jacqueline was going to picked up in the morning by her friend Jillian so they could go through their notes before the tutorials began. She was up and out of the door before Niamh had finished her breakfast.

10.30am came around so quickly as Jacqueline made her way to her private consultation with the professor in his rooms...

Her heart was melting, she contained herself and composed herself before knocking on his door. He greeted her with a big smile on his face and invited her in.

The room was so spacious it was full of books wall to wall with a big Victorian mahogany desk in the corner alcove with walnut green faux leather on the surface. A quaint vintage brass steampunk table lamp.

In the middle of the room a spacious leather chesterfield sofa, with a chesterfield armchair alongside it. In the centre of the room stood an elegant Marquetry Coffee Table with stylish open bracket legs.

As Jacqueline sat on the settee, she sank into the leather which took her breath away for a moment. The professor had already had the tea brewing and the chocolate biscuits on standby.

He began by quizzing Jacqueline on her quest at the university and what was it she wished to achieve. Jacqueline energetically explained her circumstances and couldn't stop talking her nervousness made her just spill out her life her loss and her ambition.

The professor was starry eyed by this time, he was so overcome with emotion, he almost leaned into her but courteously pulled back.

It was time to divert the conversation to essays and the professor pointed out to Jacqueline that her essay was good, but too transparent, she needed to be more specific on her argument. The hypothesis was the key to making a good essay and a good argument as it draws the reader in and makes the reader eager to read on...

She needed to work on that and do more research. All in all, he said, that she had great potential as he now flirted a little with her to see if she would reciprocate, for the professor was renowned for drawing his students in and Jacqueline was a great conquest to him as he hadn't had a student who looked so good for her age and he was eager to pursue this in more ways than one. Jacqueline hadn't encountered such mannerisms; how naïve she was... and the professor would take advantage of that in due time...

As he saw her to the door, he put his hand on her shoulder and stroked her neck to wait for a response. Jacqueline shivered for a moment and said,

'Goodbye professor, until next week'.

He gave her an alluring look and replied,

'I look forward to it, as he gazed into her eyes'.

Jacqueline slowly walked down the corridor, her face was inflamed, her mind had gone for the rest of the day, she needed to gather her thoughts...

As she arrived at the beach, she made a beeline for a secret place of thought in between Trow Rocks on the bedded seat, her place, her solitude and her thoughts.

'I must control myself and concentrate on my essay writing, I must do more research and stop all this. I am acting like a starry-eyed teenager, I am almost forty-four for goodness' sake, I must do that'

She got out her books and read and read for four hours and writing down ideas and thoughts. Her fingers were no seizing up, and she made her way back to the cottage.

'Oh! My goodness its 5.30pm! everyone will be home for their tea!

Colm left a note, 'Out at Bernadettes'

Niamh greeted her mam at the back door.

'I am just on my way-out mam; I am meeting with my peers remember'

Jacqueline was relieved! And kissed her daughter on the check,

'Enjoy yourself'

Jacqueline made herself a sandwich, for that is all she could eat, she was still numb with excitement.

Niamh made her way to the bistro and Sara and Aileen were already seated. They hugged each other.

Sara was starved she hadn't had time to eat properly at the hospital busy day.

The menu arrived and all of them were feeling quite hungry they had a feast of different dishes, beef, fish, pasta, meat dumplings and lots of chips…

Niamh couldn't wait to start the conversation, and both aunts listened with bated breath, they were astounded by the whole scenario. Sara agreed given that he has a mark around his wedding finger, Sara of all people knew what cheating was… Aileen wanted more proof so it was decided that they would gather more information.

Firstly, Niamh would try and find out where is residence was? she knew there were a few students who gossiped at lot, she would spend more time in the lunch hall as that was where the gossips gather…

Aileen would ask Arthur her husband as he knows the academics at Deeside University to see if he could shed any light of this mysterious professor and his private life…

The night had turned out to be fruitful and convincing for the way forward. Niamh did not want her mam to get hurt in any way, she has had enough sorrow in her life.

Sara changed the subject and began asking Niamh on how she was doing and how life was treating her. She probed and probed as she wanted to know more about Jack, unfortunately for her Niamh was reluctant to talk about Jack. Niamh explained that she was happy with her studies and her friends and didn't want to get involved. She was in fact in denial as she did like Jack's characteristics and his keenness not to give up on her, despite her cool attitude towards him.

Sara, however, was hopeful for Niamh, in time she will come around in her mind.

Aileen was excited about Emily and Frankie getting back from their honeymoon on Saturday as they make their new home in the Beach House.

'It will be great to have her back in the wool shop and the haberdashery, it has been challenging since she has been away', said she.

They all said their good nights and as Niamh travelled along the coast road, she began to think of her father and wished he was here. Her mind was dwindling in and out about her mam's situation, but she was clear she would find out the truth about this professor and if she is wrong, she will apologise, but her gut feeling was, she was right.

'Tomorrow is another day '……

Chapter 20

Emily and Frankie had arrived home, as they entered the Beach House there was a welcoming party there to greet them. Jacqueline, Colm and Niamh. They had arrived early to surprise them with a lovely homecoming meal for their first night in their new home.

Frankie was rather surprised to see anybody in their new home, as he looked across at Emily with a disconcerting look on his face. He quickly changed his mind when he smelt the roast beef cooking in the oven.

Jacqueline made her way towards Emily, put her arms out to give her a hug, and then responded by saying,

'We are not stopping don't worry, we just wanted to welcome you home and thought you would be in need of a good meal inside you'

Frankie folded his arms with a rather wry smile on his face as he leaned back and winked at Colm, as he whispered in his ear,

'It's nice to have company but not tonight, if you catch my drift'

Colm laughed in his ear,

'I think I do mate. Come on Mam and Niamh, you have done your bit with the lovely meal and the welcome back home, let's leave the newlyweds to it, chop! chop!'

He steered his mam through the door alongside Niamh.

'What's your hurry bro', as Niamh grabbed his arm.

'It's their time, their first night home. I bet you wouldn't want someone sitting in your house on your first night home from your honeymoon'.

Nimah shrugged her shoulders with a flippant remark,

'I doubt I will ever marry'

Colm put his hand on her arm her,

'You will our Niamh, not just yet, but you will'.

They strolled along the beach road, taking in the wispy salty air of the sea. It was only 10 minutes away from their cottage.

Jacqueline opened the gate and made her way to the kitchen as she was now feeling hungry. Niamh was happy to hear it as she had noticed that her mam was just picking at her meals these past weeks. She was hoping this was good sign that her mam was getting back to her own self. That wasn't the case as Jacqueline was upbeat, she was feeling excited as she had a secret date with the Professor in a few hours. She wouldn't have to make any excuses as she knew Niamh was out with Kate and Louise tonight and Colm was going to Bernadettes.

Colm and Niamh finally! left the house at 7pm. Jacqueline hurriedly made her way upstairs to dress up. She was meeting the Professor at the car park just a mile down the road at 8pm. As she looked in the mirror at her blue polka dress she was wearing, she sighed for a moment as she had only worn this dress once. It was four years ago…

She began to flash back to that night… Declan was wearing his navy-blue suit, white shirt and dark blue tie. They were at the Royal Hotel; it was the wedding reception of Joe and Belinda. Joe was an old school friend, and Declan was surprised to get an invitation as he hadn't seen him for years, except that one time when they greeted each other at the Newcastle football ground. Jacqueline was the one who coerced Declan to accept the invitation as she hadn't been inside the Ramsden Hotel since it had been refurbished. She wanted to go for that reason only.

Jacqueline took a moment to reminisce about that wonderful evening where she and Declan danced on the exquisite ballroom floor, it was so grand with the large crystal lights beaming down on them as the mahogany floor reflected the light. They both glided and swirled around the room like teenagers.

Suddenly! Jacqueline grasped her chest and said out loud,

'Oh, my goodness, I cannot go out, I cannot, oh No! this isn't right! Why do I feel like this! I cannot bring my love back! I must go! I promised! I don't break promises!'

She felt sick and went into the bathroom and wrenched her heart out for a few minutes.

'That's better, right, sort my face out, and get going'

It was a ten-minute walk, the fresh breeze would do her good, as she swiftly walked along the coast road. The beach lights were on, and she noticed how they glimmered and shadowed over the sandy beach, she could see footprints in the sand. She stopped for a moment, and she could see in the distance a couple walking hand in hand along the beach…

'Oh! The flash backs came flooding back. Is Declan haunting me, is he? She turned away stepped up her pace. She was almost at the car park.

The professor pulled up in his silver jaguar XJ. Jacqueline heart began to beat faster as he got out of the car, and it felt like she was still in the past. As he walked towards her she stood still for a moment to catch her breath. He slowly put his hand into hers and guided her to the car. His smile was melting Jacqueline's heart.

As they got into the car, the Professor asked Jacqueline if she would like to have dinner at his apartment which was adjacent to the university it was his rooms. Jacqueline just heard herself saying, 'yes'.

He had living accommodation that was attached to his study room. It was a large living room, with a small kitchen and bathroom, with a spacious bedroom.

The professor was so pleased that Jacqueline had accepted his invitation, as he had initiated a three-course meal to be delivered by the university restaurant staff. He had been paying certain staff generously, for some time to deliver food to his apartment on a regular basis, no questions asked. This was already in place when they got there.

They both made their way up the steps and Jacqueline made a comment,

'I had no idea you had living accommodation next to the tutorial room, how convenient for you, it must be nice to relax after a full day of teaching'

The professor nodded with a cheeky chin on his face and responded with,

'Oh, it is Jacqueline, so happy you decided to join me; you are the first women I have invited for dinner at my home'.

She was more than happy to hear that. How naïve she was, he was an outright liar, he had invited many women back to this apartment over the years, he had lost count. He had been so discreet and manipulative with certain staff, as he paid them well to keep his personal life quiet, away from prying eyes.

As they entered the living room there was stag table in the corner of the room in a secreted alcove away from the window. It had white satin tablecloth and napkins with gold banded clips. In the centre of the table was a gold candelabra with five candles to be lit...

The starters: a prawn cocktail, followed by fillet steak, new potatoes, with a salad and dressing. Dessert was Neapolitan ice cream with strawberries.

Jacqueline sat back and turned to the Professor and asked,

'Professor Macpherson, I am so impressed, do you have a housekeeper?'

He quickly shuffled towards her and engaged in the conversation,

'Please call me Alexander, we are not in class, and yes, I do have a housekeeper' as he nibbled her ear.

Jacqueline at this point was a little shaken and asked if she could use the bathroom, he escorted her to the door, as she looked aside the bedroom door was slightly ajar, and she could see the silk sheets which were the colour of champagne. They were neatly mounted on top of a mahogany bed.

She entered the bathroom, shutting the door rather abruptly which banged shut! She sat on the toilet seat not moving for some minutes. Her thoughts were in turmoil, for the first time since Declan's death she wanted to be held, she wanted to be with Alexander, his touch was a Declan touch, his smile, his walk. Why shouldn't I be loved again... She pondered and then got up to go back into the living room.

Alexander had poured two glasses of champagne and invited Jacqueline to sit on the sofa with him. He was going to take his time with Jacqueline as he knew she was not like the others, and he would patiently allure her to the bedroom later. His plan was to get Jacqueline a little tipsy so she would respond to him more effectively. He felt that this plan of action was the best plan. He proceeded...

Jacqueline sat down and took the glass of Champagne. He commented on how lovely she looked tonight.

'I am so happy you walked into my classroom; you took my breath away Jacqueline'

He put his glass down and took Jacqueline's glass out of her hand and put it down. He then bent over and put his hands around Jacqueline's face and kissed her passionately, he then proceeded to bend her back on the cushion and lay on top of her. Jacqueline at this point froze she was static with fright, as she pushed her arms upwards and made her plea!

'Please Alexander! Don't, I need to get up, I need to go, I am sorry, I am so sorry. I am so attracted to you, but I cannot do this right now please forgive me'

Alexander got up, brushed his black back hair off his face, and helped Jacqueline up off the sofa. They both faced each other, and it was Alexander who spoke first by saying,

'I apologise Jacqueline, your whole being sent my pulses racing, I got carried away with the feel of your beautiful body. I will call you a taxi darling', as he kissed her on the cheek.

Jacqueline sat on the end of the sofa and couldn't quite take in the events that had just occurred.

'He called me darling', I hadn't been called that since my Declan said it to me that night we were in bed and that was the night our Emily was conceived'.

She sat stunned and confused. Alexander stood looking out of the window for the taxi, it had arrived. He knew it wouldn't take long as the taxi service was only minutes away from the university. He was a regular with the taxi firm, again, he paid them generously for their discretion.

He said goodbye to Jacqueline on the steps, which she thought was odd. She was hoping he would go hand in hand with her to the taxi. She again, was confused with his mannerism. One minute he is so attentive and charming and loving and just then he seemed to dismiss me as if she were his housekeeper or something?

The taxi drove off and he stood at the window quite annoyed. He was hoping for a better outcome; she hadn't even finished her champagne. I must come up with a better plan than this, he was so frustrated. He decided to call one of his other women who would oblige him on his frustrations. He called old faithful, Cheryl, who was a willing student. He had his passionate night, but it was not as rewarding as he wanted. He was determined to have Jacqueline, 'patience man', as he talked to himself about her.

He would have to seduce her with his passion of literature, for Jacqueline had informed him of her passion for literature and Poetry. I must find some poetic verse to come out just at the right time... as he smiled at his image through the glass window.

Jacqueline arrived home, and found Niamh was already home, as she opened the door, Niamh came out of the kitchen.

'Hello mam, where have you been all dressed up, I have never seen you in that dress before?'

They both looked at one another and Niamh couldn't help but notice her mam looked a little stunned, a little strange.

'Are you alright mam? Do you want a cup of tea?'

'Yes, let's have a cup of tea pet. I need to tell you something'

Niamh poured the tea, and Jacqueline spilled her heart out, as Niamh tentatively listened to every word. Jacqueline omitted to tell Niamh about the passionate embraces on the sofa when he was lying on top of her, as he almost had her pants and dress off, she wasn't prepared to talk about that.

As she went onto to say how she felt like it was Declan that was touching her. Niamh was getting a little worried about her mam and these feelings, as she felt the feelings were not truly about this professor, but of her late dad.

'Mam, you are getting too close this professor. I think you should just concentrate on the subjects in class and not see him outside of class. I think that would be the best course of action. You are too confused and emotionally involved, I can see that from your reaction mam. It is not healthy mam'

Jacqueline put her hand on Niamh's and said,

'Your right pet, I am an emotional wreck right now, I need to take a step back, yes, I think you are right pet. I am glad we had this talk; you are so sensible just like your dad'

'What do you mean mam? You have always been sensible, it's just since you met this professor your sensibility has taken a different direction. You seem so erratic! And out of character all together. I have never seen you like this before mam'.

They called it a night and made their way to their beds, as the key went into the door, Colm arrived in saying, 'night, night, to them both'.

Jacqueline got undressed and got into bed, the night dreams were full of Alexander; she wasn't sure at all if she could resist Alexander the next time. She couldn't make sense of her behaviour; she only knew that she wouldn't turn down Alexander if he asked her to meet again... She knew in her heart he would...

She lay there consumed with the thought of Alexander and his passionate kisses. It was going to be a time of discretion and secrets, secrets away from her family.

Alexander however, lay in his bed thinking about Jacqueline and his biggest conquest, his ego was bigger than ever, he was determined to have her as he felt it was just a matter of time and place and planning. He decided to be cool for a week or so to see how Jacqueline responds to his coolness...

Niamh lay awake worrying about her mam; she would call on Sara and Aileen in her free period tomorrow.

'I must find out if Uncle Arthur has any news on this mystery professor. I am sure he has something to hide, the sooner we find out the better it will be for mam'

Chapter 21

Serena awoke in the early hours; the twins were awake inside of her as they fluttered away in her stomach. She became alarmed for a moment but realised it was movement, and what movers they were. She shouts out!

'Dylan! Dylan! Come out of the bathroom quick! Before you miss them! Hurry!'

Dylan ran into the bedroom and shouted!

'What! What! You are alright my love!'

Serena grabbed his hand quickly and placed it in the middle of her stomach as he felt the movement and then placed it at the right side and there another movement!

'Oh my God! This is too amazing for words; you are amazing my love! As he kissed Serena's stomach on both sides. We must get their names sorted out once in for all, no more changing our minds.

As they both sat on the bed, Serena grabbed a notebook and pen from the bedside cabinet.

'Ok, my love, my first choice for a girl's name will be Amy, and you can have first choice for the boy's name, 'Your turn now' as Dylan scratched his head and went with,

'I go with Ethan'. What if we have two girls or two boys? My second choice would be Andrew'

Serena, had already thought about that one and immediately answered,

'I love Rachel, we are now sorted'

Dylan kissed his wife on the cheeks,

'On that point I will love you and leave you, some of us have to go to work,' said he

As he arrived at work, he caught sight of Colm going towards his office and waved to him to come over.

'How are you doing lad, everything going alright from your end?'

'I am doing great Uncle Dylan, more than I can say for mam these days. So many whisperings going on between Niamh, Sara and Aileen. I think it's about this mysterious Professor. Our Niamh looks concerned, I am not sure what is behind it all. I am sure I will find out one of these days'

Dylan went on to say that Serena had mentioned she hadn't heard from Jacqueline for quite a while. She was thinking of calling her tonight to see why she hadn't been around to see her lately.

Colm thought that would be a good idea, as he felt like his mam was steering away from the family these days...

They both went their separate ways, Colm went into the Draughtsmen's office and Dylan onto the ship, 'Blue Haven' which was drydocked, it was ready for inspection.

Jacqueline had no lectures today, and she was trying to catch up with her chores at home without success as she just wanted to walk on the beach and think romantic thoughts. She was losing herself into some kind of mirror image on one side stood the Professor and on the other stood Declan which was consuming her very thought and she was so happy to let it, as she skipped lightly across the sand brushing up against her plimsoles.

The sand was damp with the misty air, but it could have been golden in Jacqueline's eyes, she was lightheaded with golden sunshine and sand. This total contrast was infectious, and it was keeping her spirits so high.

As the hours went by Jacqueline did return home and hurriedly tidied a little and made a quick tea for Colm and Niamh.

'Egg and Chips mam' as Colm looked down at it at the kitchen table thinking this is twice this week... Something isn't right here; I hope Serena calls soon and grabs mam and hopefully she will respond.

'I want my old mam back', his thoughts carried across the table to Niamh as they were both thinking the same thing.

The telephone rang, Jacqueline seemed to ignore it, as she put the kettle on. Niamh answered.

'Hello Serena, I would love to come around to see you. Yes, Mam is here I will put her on'

Jacqueline made her way to the telephone,

'Hello Serena, I am sorry I didn't call last week, so busy with studying. I will come along with Niamh, around 7pm be ok for you'

Niamh was relieved to hear that as she winked at Colm.

The car journey over to Serena's was quiet, as Niamh tried to get the conversation going about Serena and the twins, but Jacqueline gave a one-word response to everything.

They eventually arrived, Dylan opened the door to them and hugged Jacqueline, he had noticed she had lost weight and looked pale, which was worrying in his eyes.

Serena was the seated in the living room with her legs up on the pouffe, Doctors orders to keep the swelling ankles down.

Dylan made tea as they sat around Serena. It was Niamh who held all the conversation for the first ten minutes as she went through all the books Serena was reading. They engaged in all the detective stories she had read, but Serena was getting a little bored with it all and Niamh suggested perhaps she could do some knitting. Serena laughed out loud,

'Me knitting, I have never had two knitting needles in my hand ever,' said she

Nimah pointed out it was never too late. She would send Emily around this next day to sort her out. They both laughed.

Dylan took Jacqueline into the kitchen to have a word with her.

'How are you our Jacques, you look weary is everything ok?'

'Yes, Dylan, I have been studying hard, it won't be forever'

'How are the lectures, I hope the Professor is treating you well?'

Jacqueline blushed and said they should get back to Serena. She was now to engage totally on Serena to avoid any conversation about the Professor. She became animated and talking rather fast, and at times, repeating herself. Everyone had noticed that Jacqueline wasn't her true self but a mere shell that was shredding away in their eyes, but in Jacquelines eyes she was exhilarated with her new way of life.

Niamh had relayed the whole story of the Professor to Serena and that she was meeting with Aunt Aileen this next day to find out more about the mysterious Professor. Serena asked to be kept in the loop as she was worried about Jacqueline and wanted to help if her help was needed.

The night shadows were soon upon them as Jacquline took to her bed with a heavy heart, as she felt her reaction to Serena was not warranted. She was a little ashamed of herself. The empathy of joy for the forthcoming twins had deserted her. She was nonchalant at times, her loving generous heart had been stolen away and it was consumed elsewhere she couldn't stop it! She didn't want to stop it! She was keeping Declan alive, and she didn't know it, that was driving her on, and the Professor was in the driving seat.

The misty morning dew appeared, as Jacqueline looked out of her bedroom window at 6am. The mystery of it all, the shadows, those silhouette images come in and out. In the distance a captivating view of the lighthouse that stood tall as the mist suffocated the lower levels of it. It was the sunrise that flickered over the lighthouse tower breaking its way across the sea of mist with its smothering bliss.

Jacquleine was stunned by this image as it contrasted her mixed feelings of the dullness of the mist with a sun rising of bliss. She was going to be uplifted today; it was lecture of the romantic poets this morning. She learned that romantic as in the romantic movement of poets was not romance as we know it; it was an enlightening period of poets of individualism of nature and its transcendence to look beyond the mystery of creation.

The freedom to explore and navigate the written word. In effect the artistic impression that was written down in what they saw of nature, rather than romantic love. It influenced a whole new world from 1700s - 1900s. Jacqueline was elevated and fascinated by this process. She loved Keats and his poetry, his romanticism of nature and how it evolved around the aesthetics of art.

Jacqueline had read so much about it but wasn't quite sure how to evaluate such a complex subject. She was about to find out...

The lecture hall was full as usual and in walks Professor Macpherson, Jacqueline sat near the back, she felt she would blush, and others would notice her behaviour. She wanted to concentrate on what was said as this lecture was important, it was to be her favourite.

The professor's lecture was on the comparisons of the romantic poets, and what they had in common. What was their main objective, it seemed to Jacqueline that their different prefaces to art, nature and politics came down to a universal togetherness of the immortal and the imagination that transcends into truth. They were all searching for the truth.

The professor left the hall and didn't glance once at Jacqueline, he was not going to indulge today. His arrogant stance swayed out of the hall and back to his rooms. Jacqueline was relieved in one way but confused in the other.

She made her way to the restaurant and caught up with Louise who was not having a good day. She didn't enjoy that lecture it wasn't for her, and told Jacqueline she may switch modules, as he found it too complicated for her. Jacqueline was sad to hear that but if you are not enjoying it there was not much point in carrying on.

They chatted about the drama society that was starting up and Louise was going to put her name forward and asked Jacqueline if she would come along. Jacqueline declined as she felt she couldn't concentrate on anything else; she had her hands full....

As they finished their lunch and made their way to the library. The entrance to the library had revolving doors and as Jacqueline went into the right side of the doors, the Professor came out on the left side, their eyes met. The professor hurriedly ran down the stone steps leading to the grassy verge and across the pathway he made his way back to his rooms.

Jacqueline at this point was totally confused. She did not hesitate and quickly made her way to his rooms. She knocked on the door and heard a voice

'Come'

She opened the large mahogany door and as he turned his head around from his desk, he got up and walked towards Jacqueline.

'How can I help you, Jacqueline? His tone was cool and distant.

Jacqueline composed herself and realised as she stepped back and felt that decorum and civility would be the best course of action, she replied calmly,

'Yes, Professor, I would like a copy of the Romantic Poets syllabus as I appear to have misplaced mine, if that is alright Professor', she too could be a cool customer.

He was taken back for a moment and went to his cabinet to achieve the syllabus and passed it over to Jacqueline with a sly alluring look, with the hope of reciprocation which didn't appear to his annoyance when Jacqueline left the room.

He was seated with his hands on his head, confused, he was. He left his rooms to catch up with Jacqueline along the corridors and whisked her away towards the arch way, which was secluded, there was no one near the archway. He turned her head towards him desperately trying to keep some composure, but it wasn't working and began in an earnest tone,

'I must see you Jacqueline, and I know you want to see me, I can see it in your eyes'

Jacqueline gasped for a moment and raised her voice!

'I don't not know what you want you are hot and cold and distant at times; I am confused with your behaviour at times'

He brushed his black hair back from his forehead, and put his hands around Jacquelines face,

'I must see you tonight, not here, tonight at eight, come to my apartment'

Jacqueline stood for a moment and said maybe and walked away.

'Touche' as he muttered to himself, he was excited about the challenge, the challenge of having Jacqueline, it was his main objective. He was too arrogant to even contemplate that Jacqueline hadn't said yes, but maybe in his arrogant view that was a yes.

She couldn't resist, she made her way to the university and got the number 27 bus to campus at 7.30pm. As she went up to the apartment, she suddenly turned around and decided to leave. She ran and ran through campus to catch the bus back home. The emotional turmoil wouldn't give her any respite! She couldn't seem to get out of this knotted web of emotion she was having.

As she opened her front door, Aileen was on the opposite side of the door and quickly made her views known about the Professor.

'Jacqueline, I think you should know something important about Professor Macpherson. He is not what he seems, he has an estranged wife and several partners'

Jacqueline stood back and sat on the hallway chair stunned.

'How do you know all this our Aileen?'

Arthur knows some academics and I enquired, and one was only too happy to divulge his privileged behaviour. He is well known, but well protected.

'I cannot take this in, I cannot believe such a thing, he wouldn't be teaching, I think it is probably jealousy on their part as he is popular, I don't want to talk about it tonight, I am going to bed'

Niamh, Aileen and Sara sat in the living room, flabbergasted! This was going to be a hard! To protect Jacqueline. We will have to get our thinking caps on girls before he causes our Jacqueline serious emotional damage…

Chapter 22

Heavenly bliss surrounded the small beach house where Emily and Frankie had now settled in nicely, as they sat outside on the porch bench looking out at their new surroundings.

Frankie put his arm around Emily,

'This is what I always dreamed about sitting on a porch looking out at a sandy beach with the waves clustering nearby so you could hear their swooshing sound murmuring away in your ear. It's my kind of music,' said he

Emily's neck rose up slightly from her neck,

'Why Frankie Gallagher, I never knew you had such poetry in your soul, my husband! Eee! I am impressed' as she kissed him in on the lips.

Frankie replied by saying that he didn't realise it was poetry he always thought poetry was rhyming words. He laughed out loud.

They were enjoying their last day of the honeymoon atmosphere as it was back to work the next day.

Emily looked along the beach and saw Niamh and her aunties making their way to them.

'Oh! Three visitors! This sounds ominous. As Emily gave a puzzled look at Niamh as she arrived.

'Our Niamh you look complexed, something you want to tell me, I can tell by that look on your face?'

They all went into the beach house, leaving Frankie to savour the waves. Niamh began as Emily couldn't believe her ears; she thought it all rather strange. Her mam behaving in this way, she never saw this coming, not at all.

As Niamh pointed out that they all felt it was getting too involved, and they needed to catch the Professor with another woman. How they were going to do this? They hadn't figured that out yet.

Emily responded by saying that the best way would be to take her dad's old camera from the sideboard and take pictures of him and the other woman in a compromising situation. 'He would have to be all over her so mam would be convinced obviously.'

'How are we going prise the camera out of the house, you know mam, she is always looking and touching dad's things, still... I think she is beyond that our Emily; you haven't been around for the last few weeks, and she has not been herself, not even cooking or cleaning like she used to. I don't think she will miss the camera, trust me, I am right,' said Niamh.

She went on to say that she had now finished her assignments and wasn't going to be starting her next one until the following week, and she would spend the rest of the week on campus. Her excuse would be that she needed extra resources from the library.

Sara and Aileen suggested that it would be a good idea to take the camera today in readiness for any developments. They all agreed this.

Frankie entered the room and looked out of place as he stepped towards the kettle and said,

'Anyone for a cuppa'

Sara and Aileen got up to say,

'No thanks Frankie, we were just on way out. It was just a quick call to say hello'

Niamh stayed behind to speak to them both and to wish them all the happiness in their new home. She also wanted to talk to Emily about Serena and some knitting lessons. Emily was so happy about how the pregnancy was going, and she would be pleased to help.

She would call round to Serena that very afternoon with simple patterns of instruction and her demonstration of how to knit plain stitch and purl stitch to get her started.

As Niamh got up out of her chair, Emily escorted her to the back porch as they said their goodbyes.

Niamh took her time along the sandy beach as she swaggered up and down and found a stick by a jagged rock set back from the sand. She picked it up and pensively drew lines along the sand, her thoughts were staggered and jaded like the stick itself.

As she looked up at the hillside, she stood and stared for a moment as that image she was seeing was that of Jack!

'What is he doing here? It's a bit off his beaten track? He lives miles away.

Jack had spoken to Colm that very morning and he knew exactly where Niamh would be, and he had every intention of catching up with her. He was a determined young man, so smitten was he.

He had caught sight of Niamh and jumped quickly down the steep beachy steps; he was next to her within minutes.

'Why are you panting Jack?'

'Well! I have just jumped down 40 beachy steps to get here so yes, I am a little out of breath'

Niamh candidly smirked with curiosity as she had never seen that before.

'Are you laughing at me Niamh?'

'I am not laughing at you Jack. I am curious as to why you are here and why jump those steep steps, you could have broken your neck'

'Would you have comforted me, if I had?'

'I don't know, maybe?'

'You are hard work, Niamh Gibson, that's for sure, but you are worth it'

Niamh's eyes widened like golf balls she was shocked but rather impressed with such a bold statement.

They walked along the beach together. Jack was almost touching her hand but wasn't sure if Niamh was willing to touch his. They walked closely together as he started the conversation.

'How is the teaching course going? I bet you will be glad when it's all done and dusted so you can get to your dream job?'

Niamh smiled at Jack and responded by saying,

'I am doing well, it's just six weeks away for final assignments, and yes, I will be very happy'.

'Could I ask if you would be free for drinks on Saturday night', as he eagerly awaited her reply.

Niamh looked at Jack's face and couldn't say no, as he looked so willing to please her. She hadn't given Jack a good time these past weeks, as she didn't want to explain what had transpired about the mysterious Professor and her mam. That was a family matter only.

He left the beach a happy man and kissed Niamh on her on the cheek, as he merrily stepped briskly up those beachy steps whistling away with such energy in his legs.

Her mind drifted back to her mam as she went into the cottage via the back garden. Her mam wasn't in to her dismay.

She hurried to the telephone table and picked her bag and car keys and drove to the campus. Niamh wanted to make headway into the Professor's private life, and she knew where to go first.

There was a group of students in the library on the top floor. Niamh quietly grabbed some books, not even looking at the titles and sat in the booth behind them, as she could hear every word.

As she opened the first book it was book of history depicting the first world war. As the group began to whisper Niamh quickly pulled her chair to the side to get some understanding of what they were talking about.

One student began by saying,

'Oh! that Cheryl, she is something else, have you heard the latest about her and Professor Macpherson, she is always at his rooms and comes out in the early hours, so they say?'

Another student responded,

'She has moved on to another. I think she is trying to score points with her degree. They say she makes a beeline for several of the lecturers. Sush, here she comes, don't say a word...'

In walked a tall blonde leggy girl with a low-cut top and mini skirt with high heel boots.

'Hiya everyone, how you are doing', as she swayed her hips back and forth.

Niamh was cross with herself as she hadn't taken the camera with her... She was sure alright that she would be able to recognise her again, who could miss her! Niamh got a good look at her. She couldn't help but notice as the conversation got underway with the rest of the students that Cheryl portrayed herself by being rather manipulative, and they say that she was quite intelligent with it. Why would she give herself in that way to someone like that sleazy Professor. It was beyond comprehension in Niamh's eyes.

She would telephone Sara and Aileen as soon as she arrived home. Aileen answered the ringing telephone, she was rather surprised at such an early outcome, as she listened tentatively to what Niamh was saying.

'I think we need to do a spot of surveillance outside the Professor's apartment, don't' you?' said Aileen.

'Yes, I do Aunt, I think it's time now'

Aileen suggested that they use her car to camp out for the night; a Honda as it had lots of room to stretch, and they could take turns of grabbing some light sleep, as it may be long night... She would call Sara right away.

Unknown to them all, Jacqueline was having a rendezvous with the Professor that very night as they were having drinks out. His plan was to lure her back to the apartment.

Niamh was under the impression that her mam was with Louise studying as that was what she had been told...

It was now 7.30pm and Aileen arrived at the cottage along with Sara to pick up Niamh. Aileen had packed lots of drinks and snacks for them all and there were blankets in the boot if needed.

It was gloomy drizzly night, as they parked up at the side of the apartment just on the corner out of sight, but they could get a glimpse of the comings and goings. It was fortunate for them all to see a night light shining on his porch at the front.

'How kind of him to leave us some light', as Aileen sneered with distaste for this man.

Niamh asked Sara and Aileen what their husbands thought about them staying out all night.

Sara said that John understood why she was doing this, well, he couldn't be opposed to it, given his history... and in fact he was so happy that they had got passed their awful ordeal.

Aileen looked at Sara and conveyed her views,

'Your John is a saint compared to this man, in my view. My Arthur thinks it would be a good thing to get concrete evidence of this man's wrong doings as he has got away with so much in the past, and no one seems to be bothered about it as they are paid generously not to say anything'.

Sara nodded a yes, and Niamh agreed with her.

They had sat for a few hours and drank plenty of coffee and snacks to keep them going. Aileen was the first to shut her eyes at 10.30pm.

Niamh saw headlights coming in their direction and signalled to Sara just to duck her head down slightly. Aileen was already rested back, snoring slightly...

To Sara's shock and dismay, it was her sister Jacqueline who got out of the car first. The Professor opened the door to let her out of the car and as they made their way to the front door, Sara nudged Aileen sharply in the ribs.

'What, what, yea, yea, as she sniggered and murmured'

She opened her eyes, and they all stared at the front door as the professor had his arm around Jacquelines waist...

Niamh, got a bit emotional with her outburst,

'That's my mam, I am going in to get her, I am!'

Sara held her back and forcefully spoke out,

'You cannot do that Niamh; she is a grown woman, and she would not thank you for it. Let's just wait and see, hopefully she won't stay long, and we can get him another day...'

Jacqueline didn't take her jacket off this time and declined a coffee as she wanted to talk to the Professor about the rumours of other women and his wife.

He was so good at composing himself. It was like listening to a completely different man as he slickly explained that he was in the middle of divorce proceedings. A complete lie of course. The rumours of other women were complete fabrication as he explained his passion for learning and his extracurricular lessons. He honestly believed his own lies. Jacqueline was taking it all in with such relief and hope. She tentatively looked at his features and mannerism, it was like she was sitting in the room with Declan, her heart began to melt again.

She was happy with the response and decided to have a coffee with him. He didn't make a move on her as he was hoping she would make the first move.

As time lapsed Jacqueline got up to say goodnight, and the Professor offered to give her lift home as he hadn't been drinking alcohol. He was easing himself in with Jacqueline, and in his view, it was working. He couldn't help but notice the sparkle in Jacqueline's eyes, as he menacingly looked into her eyes with such vulgarness...

The girls tentatively watched the clock and the door as it opened and the sigh of relief on Niamh's face was a picture. He opened the car door for Jacqueline.

'Aw well! He has some chivalry of a kind. a sort of gentleman like manner, even if it's just opening the car door for a lady' said Aileen...

They sat for a while and drove home...

Chapter 23

It was beginning to feel like summer as the month of May begins to flower around the beautiful landscape of gardens along the coast road. That feeling of new beginnings seemed to be in the air... In Jacqueline's case it felt like a romantic illusion as she flew the curtains back and opened the window to feel the glorious rays of sunshine on her face. She felt the smell of her roses in the garden below, and glanced up to the still whisper of the calm sea beyond...

'Oh, sea of beauty, my compass, my peace, cometh with your quiet release'

Jacqueline stood stagnated, still as a statue, she felt the image of Declan upon her and clasped her breast tightly with such strength, she was bruising herself. Suddenly! She shook herself back to reality and moved quickly to the bathroom and forgot this mysterious incident as if it had never happened. She wasn't going to be consumed with the past in her mind, but she couldn't escape it.

Emily was at the front door to check on her mam, as Niamh had spoken to Emily on the previous night. Niamh and Emily chatted in the living room before the door opened and Jacqueline appeared, dressed, ready for the day of studying. The course was due to finish, and she wanted to get the best out of it.

'Hello Mam, just called in before I make my way to Serena's, just wanted to say a quick hello as I haven't seen you in a while mam. You must come round for tea this week. How about tomorrow mam, I am cooking a dinner, just how you taught me, so you can be my judge and jury, don't be shy mind, just say it as it is, ha ha' as Emily tried to add a bit of humour to the situation...

Jacqueline smiled at her daughter and agreed to have tea with her, yes, she hadn't seen her for a while. They talked about the course but omitted to mention the Professor. Emily could see that her mam was animated about passing her course and hoped the situation with the Professor was just a phase. She wasn't at all concerned as she thought her mam's constitution was far too strong to let a romantic episode affect her…

Niamh, however, was not of that opinion at all, and she was determined to expose the Professor once in for all...

Emily left the house and made her way to Serena's. She had a box full of patterns; first step patterns for the beginners and lot of wool and some crochet and cross stitch instructions for beginners.

Serena was excited to see Emily, as she looking forward to a new adventure, whilst she awaited the birth of the twins, which was some months away…

They sat in the summer house with the doors and windows open to take in that beautiful summer air and sunshine.

A pot of tea was made, and plate of shortbread was placed on the beautiful mosaic table with well-placed white laced mats for the cups, saucers and tea plates. Serena was so co-ordinated and stylish. Emily looked on with admiration and she knew which patterns to pick out for Serena.

'I think we should start with a something small and simple to get you into the rhythm of knitting. These are your needles, and I will start you off with how to do a plain stitch. We attach the wool onto the needle by tying a knot, so we have our loop effect. We then place the right-hand needle into the loop, go under the needle and pull your wool over, draw the needle out and there is your first stitch'

'Oh my, this looks rather good Emily', as she takes her chunky wooden needles, and chunky yarn'

It wasn't long before Serena found this very relaxing.

'It is now time to show you the purl stitch. The needle enters from the top to the bottom. Insert the right needle downwards through the front of the first stitch with the wool in front, wrap it anticlockwise around the tip of the right needle, with the tip of the right needle draw a loop by going up through and out of the left stitch, bringing the right needle away from you. This will create a bobble pattern effect which I think you will like.

Serena was finding this a little tricky now as she fumbled a little with this one.

'I prefer the plain stitch, but I will persevere with this one '

They laughed and carried on for a quite a while and Serena had finished her first piece of work, it looked rather like a small handkerchief.

'This is a challenge, but I am always up for a challenge,' said Serena.

They chatted about tapestry and crochet and cross stitch; Emily would leave the instructions and all the thread and thimbles for Serena to explore.

The conversation turned to the twins and Serena was happy to talk about them as she was so looking forward to seeing them in a few months. She explained to Emily that she needed to keep her blood pressure under control, and she felt that the knitting process would be a great way to relax; a therapy of calm is what she needed.

Serena enquired about the family and Emily made a short response about her mam and the Professor and shut it down before Serena could enquire more about it. She instead talked about Niamh and Jack and how they were getting on well together these days.

It was as if Emily was avoiding the subject of her mam and the Professor she didn't want to believe it, and if she didn't talk about it very much, she wouldn't believe it.

Emily would leave the patterns and all the accessories with Serena, and she would pop back to see her work later in the week.

They said their goodbyes, and as Serena made her way back to the summerhouse, she couldn't help but think about Jacqueline, as she was very fond of her.

'I will call Niamh soon to see how things are going', as she murmured away.

Serena got on well with Niamh and it would be best to talk to her rather than directly to Jacqeline, these were her thoughts as she sat and poured another cup of tea'

Emily made her way to her haberdashery shop. She couldn't believe how the wool and haberdashery shop had expanded as she was running out of space for everything.

Her ideas turned to art as she felt that the portraits of tapestry and cross stitch could be implemented into a small art shop next door, as her ideas flowed liked the river. She smiled at herself in the car mirror as he had pulled up outside the shops.

Her thoughts quickly turned to her mam and the Professor.

'I hope Niamh's over reaction is not true' she said to herself. She knew in her heart that her sister was not prone to overreacting...

Niamh was studying hard that morning, her final assignments were due in mid-day. She couldn't wait to get them done and make her way over to the dormitories. She wanted to find out more about this Cheryl, as she felt she was key to the Professor's downfall...

As she entered the quaint bookshop opposite the dormitory she was in luck, for there seated in the corner booth was Cheryl with some of her fellow students. Niamh took her place at the nearby bookshelf pretending to browse through the books whilst tentatively listening to the conversation, she even tilted her body slightly to hear more effectively, as if she was pulling out an awkward book stuck on the shelf. Her stance was not exposing her as she was able to hear every word...

'I am having my tutorial at six with the Professor,' said Cheryl
Maxine, her fellow student replied,

'Is that what you call it, you had your essay tutorial yesterday, this must be the exploring tutorial' as Maxine smirked back at Cheryl

'Oh, I don't know what you mean, he does like to explore me a lot, a very lot. I cannot help it if I am irresistible'

She smiled back at Maxine with a rather competitive smile as if to say, I am the one, the only one. She had no idea how cruel the Professor was...

Niamh knew she would have to be cruel to be kind where her mam was concerned, she would have to find a way to get her to the campus at six, it was the only way to expose him.

'I will speak to Sara and Aileen; Oh No! Sara she is on duty at the hospital and Aileen is in Edinburgh today! Oh! Well! I will do this myself'

She pondered and pondered and as she looked up at the notice board, she saw a printed flyer'

'Poetry recital tonight at seven, Evette Stringer one of the students in her mam's class. She will be reciting her poem, 'Oak Tree'

'That's this! Got it! Mam will come for she loves poems of nature'

She made her way to the library as it was 2pm and she knew her mam would be there as she always spends a few hours in the afternoon in the library.

As she went through the revolving doors and up the stairs, she caught a glimpse of the Professor talking to her mam. She shivered with fright; she wasn't expecting him to be here. Her walk towards them was a walk of deliberation, for Niamh would prise her away without a further thought.

'Hi mam, glad I caught you, just need a quick chat if that's alright'

The Professor gave Niamh an alluring smile.

'Hello Niamh, lovely to see you again…', as he put his hand out to shake Niamh's. He left his hand in hers too long in Niamh's eyes as she pulled away from him...

'I shall see you tomorrow Jacqueline for your final papers to put forward, you will pass with flying colours I have no doubt about that'.

He glanced swiftly at Niamh as he passed her on his way out of the library.

'Mam, you never guess who is reciting poetry here at six, its Evette from your class, and I think we should both go, don't you' as Niamh eagerly awaited her reply...

'Oh, right, I didn't know, yes, we should, I am so happy for her, she will be heard. I hope there is a good crowd that attends'

'We can have tea here mam, it's just a couple of hours away'. Let's go to the Lantern, I love that small cupboard of express meals that you can just take from the trolley and eat on the stoney mounted seats outside, it's so rustic, let's do that'

Time went by so quickly and as they had finished their mixture of sandwich, salad and chips. Niamh looked up as she placed the food papers in the bin annexed, she caught sight of Cheryl moving towards the Professor's apartment.

'Oh mam, let's walk off all the food we have just eaten, it was lovely. The grounds here so idyllic with these glorious trees and shrubbery and artefacts planted on each verge of green, its magnificent.

Jacqueline agreed and as they took the pathway at the back of the apartment, Jacqueline stood still like a frozen portrait. For behind a shrub on the back wall was the Professor and Cheryl, he had his hands on her bottom, pressing her into him and he was passionately kissing her. He grabbed her hand and took her quickly in through the back door…

Jacqueline couldn't move, didn't say a word, didn't make a sound, as she sat on the grass. She couldn't take it in, she didn't want to take it in.

Niamh sat on the grass with her mam and said,

'I knew this was happening; I had to get you here mam so you would believe me'

Jacqueline turned to her daughter with a frozen expression on her face, and quite calmly spoke,

'I am glad you did, I am glad, I am. I have been a complete fool; I have humiliated myself and I have soiled your dad's memory'

'Mam, you didn't have sex did you with this man?'

'No, I thought about it, but no, I am so pleased I didn't', as she cried with tears of relief rather than sadness'

'Listen to me Mam, listen to me, you have not soiled Dad's memory, you have not. You were taken in by his resemblance of Dad, you just got carried away with the creation of Dad and seemingly thought you had found someone so like him. He is not!

Jacqueline put her arm around and reciprocated triumphantly,

'He certainly isn't'. She began to laugh out loud with joy and pain and tears.

They both jumped up, and Jacqueline began to say,

'Let's go hear Evette and her poem about the Oak Tree'

They sat in small hall which was at the back of the Chapel as they listened to Evette as she made the poem about the Oak Tree come alive with its drooping bow; the poem was in three parts which covered the seasons of change, it was refreshing and light. They both transcended for a while it became a good distraction. The applause was well deserved for Evette.

They left the campus, and Niamh drove slowly back along the beach as they took in the sequences of change, as the beachy head looked spritely and alert as if it knew summer was on its way.

As they both got out of the car and took a little stroll along the beachy head as they watched the sea unfold.

'You alright mam?'

'Yes, I am fine pet, I will get my degree and be out of there. I have neglected my family a little, it's time I got back to the real me again'

'You haven't really mam, and this is the real you, the new you. Just think of it as a learning curve as you have loved the process and enjoyed the lectures, and you have attained so much knowledge Mam. You must not let go of it, you just let go of the romantic episode, for it was just an episode, a blip in your life'

'Well put my pet, yes, well put, I will think on that'

As Jacqueline took to her bed, she unravelled her heavy heart, and began thinking of Declan, and how she felt alive again, but she knew in her heart that it is memories and memories alone will keep her alive. She will be satisfied with that as she put her head on her pillow and slept….

Chapter 24

The next day was full of unrest and anxious moments as Niamh preceded downstairs awaiting anxiously for her mam to appear. She was hoping that her mam was in good spirits, but she knew her mam, it must have been such a shock for her to find that the Professor was a liar and a cheat.

The moment arrived and her mam appeared looking pale and tired.

'Cup of tea mam, I have just put the kettle on' as Niamh looked pensively on towards her mam.

'Oh, that's lovely pet, let's get today over with. I just need to get my results, and I will be out of the university before you can say, Abra gad Dabra!'

They both drank their tea and grabbed their bags. Niamh quickly picked her keys up and ushered her mam into the car.

'What a lovely day, I don't think I have seen such a lovely sky, and those clouds resonating over the sea hovering over the sea like a mother sound, and moving quietly over the misty spray...'

Jacqueline seemed to go into a trance as she wasn't listening to Niamh who was saying that she would drop her off and make her way to the teaching college. She would be about an hour or two before she could return to pick her mam up.

'Mam! I am talking to you; didn't you hear a word I said'

'Oh! Sorry pet, I was miles away enjoying the beautiful view. What was it you were saying?'

Niamh repeated herself and her mam was fine about it, as she was going to the chapel to light a candle after her results. She felt such an urge to light a candle in memory of Declan her mind and her thoughts did not leave her head. It was consumed with Declan.

They had arrived at the university and Jacqueline made her way to the big hall to get her results. She spotted her dear friends Louise and Jillian. They all decided to meet up after wards for a cup of coffee.

As they waited patiently to receive that important brown envelope. The hall got very busy, and everyone was pushing and shoving, and Jacqueline lost sight of Jillian, she could just see Louise in the distance,

Finally, she had received her important envelope, and it was good news she had passed with excellent marks. She had mixed emotions; a feeling of such joy, coupled with a feeling of sorrow; suddenly she felt overwhelmed and rushed out of the hall, to get some fresh air, as she couldn't catch her breath.

She walked towards the seated area near the big oak tree and sat to gather her emotions. It was then when she looked up from her results, the Professor stood there tall and handsome with a sultry look on his face.

'Jacqueline, so glad I caught you, we must talk, I must explain a few things to you. It wasn't as it seemed yesterday'

Jacqueline looked up at him with a stoney expression on her face and gave him a stern stony reply.

'Oh! Yesterday that is old news, I must dash, as I have an appointment. It was nice seeing you, and I enjoyed the course, but it's over now, and I have better things to think of now. Good day Professor'

She walked with her head high, and she strode along the path as if she were on a march parade. She left the professor, still, shocked and amazed at what he had just witnessed. He shook his head with arrogance and disdain and walked back into the hall.

Jaqueline shook with emotion and made her way into the chapel; she sat for over an hour after she had lit a candle. She recited the Haily Mary ten times and went through her rosary as she knelt looking up at the virgin Mary (Our Lady). Her mind became peaceful and serene and as she got up to go, Fr Donnelly appeared as he made his way to where she was seated.

'Hello Jacqueline, it has been a while since I have seen you, I was at the point of giving you an unexpected visit at home dear'

Jacqueline began to cry, and Fr Donnelly gave her his handkerchief to blow on. It was then that Jacqueline began to unfold all the happenings that had gone by. She asked for confession, as she felt that she had sinned against Declan's memory, but she hadn't, it made her feel better to tell Fr Donnelly all.

He listened patiently to her plight and gave her the Act of Contrition of just three hail Mary's. Jacqueline felt that her penance should have been at least five or more.

He went on to say that it would perhaps be beneficial to Jacqueline if she went on a retreat a little break from it all. He could organise a retreat St Josephs for three days for her if she felt it would help her.

Jacqueline sat quietly for a moment and replied.

'You know Father, I think you may be right, that is just what I need. St Joseph's was further down the coastline, but it wasn't that far away, ten miles or so.

'Just so you know Jacqueline, there is no smoking and drinking at the convent, but you probably already knew that' as Father Donnelly smiled back at Jacqueline.

'I like a glass of wine with my sisters, but I can well do without for a few days I am sure Father'

'There will be lots of activities beside solitude and prayer; the sisters and monks are very talented in their approach to needlework, painting and arts and crafts; it will be beneficial to you Jacqueline. I think you need a bit of respite dear; it will do you good'

Jacqueline felt a light had been lit in her life at that moment and she thanked Father Donnelly for this happy interruption of which she needed...

She made her way to the library and awaited Niamh's return. Louise and Jillian were seated in the Foyer.

'Where have you been Jacqueline, we were waiting on you for drinks', said Jillian

'I am so sorry girls, I am meeting up with my daughter Niamh, she is on her way, you go off and enjoy. I am so happy for you both, congratulations on your results. We can catch up soon,' said Jacqueline.

They both looked at Jacqueline, a little put out, as they walked away.

It wasn't long before Niamh appeared radiant and so excited. She too, had receiving great news, her teaching degree was a first class one, she couldn't believe it, as she was sure she would get a second-class degree.

They sat in the foyer, hugging each other and Jacqueline turned to her daughter.

'I need to talk to you about something, not here, we can talk at home'

Niamh looked concerned.

'Why mam, what is it, why not here, please you are alarming me mam'

'Oh! Pet, its nothing to be alarmed about I assure you'

They both made their way to the car park and Niamh, questioned her mam once again.

'Let's just enjoy the ride home along the coast road, it's such a lovely day. We can put the kettle on and then we can talk my pet'

The journey seemed to take a long time in Niamh's eyes, but it was only a ten-minute drive. She couldn't wait to get in the house and put the kettle on.

'Right mam, let's have it, out with it'

'Right pet, I bumped into Father Donnelly at the Chapel and we both agreed I would go on a retreat for three days next week to St Joseph's Convent. I need to be by myself for a while, please understand'

Niamh sat her mam down and held her hand.

'I do understand mam, you have always been so strong and there for us all, and I think it would do you good. You are the one with the strong faith, and you have been away from it for a while, it probably is time for you to reconnect with your faith mam'

Jacqueline hid her real thoughts and emotions well; she always kept them under lock and key. The scenario with the Professor had taken its toll and the release of it all would come out eventually, she wanted to do this on her own. St Josephs was in a quiet reclusive spot along the coastline, as it is set back with lovely gardens all around.

Niamh left her mam to her thoughts, as she was to meet up with Kate and Jessica, as they were having a celebratory lunch at the Lantern.

As she arrived at the Lantern, the girls were already seated with a drink already bought for Niamh. They all jumped up with joy and shouted

'Yes! We did girls, we bloody did it! Despite everything! Yes!'

They partied with the rest of the campus; it was a lively at the Lantern on this sunny afternoon.

Kate and Jessica quizzed Niamh about Jack, but she was keeping her thoughts close to her chest, and they wouldn't let go until they could prise this vital information out of her.

Kate was up first.

'Come on Niamh, we share, we care, come on now, we would share'

'Oh! Alright! Already! I am seeing Jack later to drinks, yes, we are getting on so well, he is so caring and mature, not what I thought at all, and he is patient with me'

Jessica had a tear in her eye as she turned to Niamh

'Oh mate, I think that is wonderful I do, you deserve such happiness, you do'

Niamh quickly responded,

'You do my dear friend, and now you have this placement coming up, you too deserve much happiness. Let's go with happiness and success'

They all clinked their glasses together, 'Happiness and success'

They vowed to keep in touch with each other no matter where they end up.

The afternoon went by so quickly and Niamh had to hurry home to get change as she will be running late at this rate. She kissed her friend's goodbye.

Jack was at the door, prompt at 7.00pm and Niamh managed to get herself dressed to impress. She was so excited to share her news with Jack, her heart was beating fast now. The doorbell rang and Jack stood in his navy jersey cardigan and polo neck jumper underneath, he looked very smart with his casual look.

Niamh wore her white chiffon blouse with blue polka dots and her best navy-blue slacks with navy blue ballerina shoes.

'Wow! You look smashing lass, absolutely smashing' as Jack stared at her with such admiration. Let's go girl, we can stop off at the bistro first and go on to Gray Hat if you fancy, music later'

They sat in the bistro and Jack was overwhelmed with Niamh's success; he was feeling a little out his comfort zone. His thoughts began to drift in and out and he started to wonder if Niamh was too good for him, it was unsettling him a little bit.

Niamh, however, was getting to really like Jack and she started to show a little more interest him as she was interested in his work as a trainee manager at the pit, it reminded her of her dear dad Declan.

The night turned out to be eventful especially when they arrived at the Gray Hat. Some of Jack's friends arrived and teased him about getting hooked up with Niamh.

Niamh was introduced to his friends who were so complimentary to Niamh and joked about Jack being a skin flint with his money, he was part Scottish they said, on his dad's side.

'I hope you got your purse with you hinny, you might need it' as they jokingly teased Jack about his moth balls in his pocket.

That was soon remedied as Jack paid for a whole round and they all cheered, it had done this in the past, but the lads enjoyed teasing him.

It was at that moment Niamh started to enjoy yourself with Jack's friends. Steve brought along his girlfriend Elaine who was a hairdresser in local salon. You could tell her hair was immaculate; a French bun that stood up with such precision and care. They were getting on so well and they all danced the night away.

As the night closed Jack left his car in the car park and booked a taxi home, as he saw Niamh to the door, he put his hands around her face and kissed her passionately before saying

'You are amazing lass, an absolute bobby dazzler'

Niamh stood mesmerised that kiss was so meaningful, and she reciprocated and responded

'You lad, are a game changer, you have brought me back to life, you do know that'

Niamh skipped into the cottage as she waved Jack goodbye, singing all the way up the stairs.

Jacqueline was half awake, still feeling the effects of the day, her heart was wrenched and bruised.

'How could have fallen for such a wretched creature, I was blinded, he was nothing like Declan at all!'

She prayed for peace and solace within her, as she declared her determination to get back to normal and phase out this terrible episode in her life.

The darkness fell upon the sky and nightfall had settled in....

Chapter 25

It was a day of dismay and turmoil at the University. The day of reckoning had occurred… as the Professor was confidently, gathering up all the exam papers and coursework papers. He always put them in a cordial chronological order, for he was renowned for his pedantic mannerisms; a man who believed he was picture perfect in every aspect of his working and personal life, so assured of himself, but he was in for a shock today…

A sudden loud bang on the door.

'Come in!' said the professor

The Dean entered the room, he was accompanied by a tall well-dressed man in a grey suit and grey trilby which was slightly tilted on his head, alongside him was uniformed police constable

As the Professor got up out of his chair rather coyly with his eyebrow raised.

'What can I do for you gentleman, has there been an incident on campus?'

The man in the grey suit, Detective Inspector Gilmore responded in his direct way.

'Yes, there has been an incident, a very serios allegation has come to my attention which involves you Sir. You are acquainted with a certain Cheryl Lansbury are you not?'

'I certainly am, she is a student of mine' said the professor in a rather confident manner.

'I am here to inform you that due to the severity of the incident, we ask you to come quietly to the station for further questioning'

'Am I under arrest Inspector?'

'No, we merely asking for your co-operation in this matter, if you would like to step this way, and the Constable will escort you to our vehicle outside'

The professor was not amused, but he knew if he didn't co-operate it would look guilty as charged. He grabbed his coat and marched out of the door with the constable at his side.

They arrived at the police station and the Professor was ushered into interview room 2. He was left there for some time and was getting rather impatient.

The door opened and in walked the Inspector accompanied by a Detective Sergeant Milrose.

They were all seated, and the Inspector read out his rights and began by displaying a folder full of evidence of the allegation, which included some vivid photographs and Miss Lansbury's account of the incident.

'On the night in question, Saturday 5 June you did vehemently allure Miss Lansbury to your apartment with the intent of having intimate relations with her?'

The Professor portrayed a false look of anguish and surprise to affect his so-called innocence.

'I don't know why she would say such a thing, I know sometimes students do fantasise about their lecturers, it comes with the job Inspector'

The Inspector displayed the six black and white photographs. He spread them out across the desk slowly and calmly so the Professor could take a long look at them all.

The first three photographs show passionate embraces between the two parties just outside the apartment.

The other three photographs show in graphic detail the images of sexual intercourse taking place.

The professor looked on with horror and despair, he quickly replied by nervously saying

'I wish to call my Solicitor, right now! Right now!'

'I bet you do sir,' said the Inspector.

The Inspector and the Sergeant left the room, as they walked down the corridor, Sergeant Milrose grinned,

'We have him bang to rights Sir, don't we'

The Inspector rapidly responded

'Oh, he will get his Solicitor in and come up with some bizarre explanation that the poor girl was the predator, and he was the victim, he looks that type to me, so privileged and arrogant with it'

Cheryl got her revenge, she planned the evening in question with such detail, as her fellow student, Timothy who had a crush on her was happy to fulfil her requests to take photographs. As

Timothy Crouched down under the bedroom window. He was aware that Cheryl would slide the curtain back to make just enough for him to catch the Professor in the act. Although, he wasn't expecting such intimate photographs but took them anyway. Photography was his passion, and he was totally taken in by Cheryl's persuasion and flirting; she hadn't paid him that much attention before and he liked it.

The outcome was not what the Professor was expecting, he was delusional to think that such damming evidence would get him off Scott free. He couldn't understand where these photographs came from.

His career at the University was over and he was charged and bound over for inappropriate behaviour in a workplace.

An agreement was reached between the parties whereby the Professor would generously recompense Miss Cheryl Lansbury to the sum of £1,000.00. She was happy with that; her intentions were solely to humiliate the Professor as he did her. She was more than happy to take the money.

Cheryl was a flamboyant soul, with no scruples or morals really, she used people and poor Timothy got put on the sidelines too. Her next venture was to find herself a millionaire to devour. She believed in herself.

It wasn't long before the news reached the campus and Niamh shortly after received the news. She was pleased about the news but was reluctant to divulge it to her mam.

Jacqueline was on her way to her retreat and Niamh wasn't going to spoil her mam's solace.

The journey to St Joesph's was serene, a steady coach ride. Jacqueline sat near the back and admired the view as the coach seemed to go rather slowly. The coastline was supreme with its long sandy beaches that seem to go on forever. It was soothing sight.

As the coach pulled up in the lovely courtyard. To the left of the courtyard stood flowerbeds and shrubs solidly erect among the lengthy grassy verges; the size was measured out to perfection, its precise symmetrical square and its paved mosaic walkway all around gave it that majestic look. Jacqueline felt like she had stepped into a new timeline, the Jacobean era, it took her breath away as she stood with a surreal look upon her face.

Brother Thomas in his brown robe and Sister Clarice in her neatly attire; a black and white habit. They came towards Jacqueline to welcome her to St Josephs. Brother Thomas took her bags and escorted her to her quarters, her cell for three days. She would be placed next to Sister Catherine, a small chubby nun, with big rosy cheeks and a big smile.

Jacqueline moved towards the stairs, and she was on the first floor. As she stopped outside her door Sister Catherine came out of her cell and spoke energetically to Jacqueline.

'Welcome my dear, now you get settled in, and if you need anything night or day, I am next door. We are all assembled in the crafts hall this afternoon, as some of the sisters are knitting and cross stitch is also taking place.

We do have some brothers who are keen painters and there are lots of books to read. If you prefer a spot of gardening Sister Bridget would be more than happy to oblige you. Prayers at five take place in the chapel'

It was to be an interesting phase in Jacqueline's life, and she was keen to embrace it all. She got herself settled and prayed to our lady before leaving her cell, and she then made her way to the crafts hall.

The hall was solid oak with high ceilings and old-fashioned chandeliers were perched delicately on the ceiling with brassy chains that looked like they had been seated there for a lifetime.

The long benches were full of articles and accessories in readiness for the activities and Jacqueline was hoping to learn some cross stitch as she hadn't done that before.

It so happened that sister Luke was the master, and she would sit with Jacqueline as she gave her a small piece of cloth to practice on. It was a small dove she was hoping to achieve on her small cloth, it didn't quite go to plan at first, but after a couple of hours she seemed to be getting the hang of it.

As she got up to flex her fingers and have a walkabout, she couldn't help but notice the poetry books of several centuries. Jacqueline happened on the great poet *'Gerard Manley Hopkins' a poem, 'Spring and Fall'* Jacqueline was consumed with the, it reminded her of human experiences. It reflected her human experience of joy and pain. It seemed to comfort her in some way.

Sister Luke came over to her and spoke with a gentle voice,

'Dear child, you are an ardent reader, that is an enjoyable pastime in itself'

Jacqueline looked caringly at Sister Luke,

'It is Sister, it is one of my great comforts in life, I love to read and write too'

'You must explore your writing child while you have the time here, for there is much to see and much to write about'

Jacqueline felt a sudden relief of such energy in her soul she hadn't had for a long time, she felt ten years younger.

She enjoyed her lesson of cross stitch, but she felt the urge to write and write… and began a spiritual poem of her own.

Thee of little faith, oh God why must this be so
Thee must call to thy inner spirit to shine through
Thy faith is strong within, thee..
Thy deepest fears are not wanted
Sweep aside and thee will see…

That moment Jacqueline felt a total transformation had come over, she was complete, she was strong, she was at peace with herself and with God. This visit to St Josephs, would stay with her for the rest of her life she felt it and was totally engaged in the process.

A light was lit and the foggy image she had sustained since the death of Declan had disappeared. She could see quite clearly her future, her life. Her thoughts diverted to teaching and those who were underachieving across the curriculum. She would enquire about Teaching Centres, for the young and the old when she returned.

In the meantime, Brother Jacob, was keen to show off his paintings. He was the joker of all the brothers with his outgoing personality, his joyous and exuberant persona resonated throughout the hall.

It was almost time for Chapel and the mood was sombre and sedate; the rosary was recited and Brother Jacob, persuaded Jacqueline to read at Mass the next morning. She was a little apprehensive, but she couldn't say no to Brother Jacob with his puppy dog eyes.

Jacqueline slept soundly that night in her cell and was ready for her reading at Mass. Brother Jacob coached her

'Shout it out dear Jacqueline, shout it out as if you mean it'

She took his advice and felt the strength of the word so profoundly within her, she was invigorated, it was if she was reborn again. It felt so satisfying and pleasing to the soul. No more thoughts of despair or negativity, just a positive force that she wanted to bottle and keep forever.

Jacqueline made a deal with herself for whenever she felt her mood was slipping, she would pull out a memory from St Josephs to guide her back to a positive place.

Her time at St Josephs had come to end and Father Donnelly happened to visit on her departure as he had planned it, so he could take Jacqueline home. He was so happy to hear that it all went well for her, it was one his best ideas yet, he thought to himself...

As they ventured along the coastline, Jacqueline was full of animated conversation, Father Donnelly was not expecting that kind of transformation but was happy to listen to all. He was well acquainted with the brothers and sisters at the convent and knew Father Jacob wouldn't disappoint.

It was the most pleasant journey either of them had experienced and as Father Donnelly got close to the cottage, Niamh was making his way down the path of the cottage, as she turned to close the gate, she caught a glimpse of the car and was so pleased to see her mam back.

As Jacqueline got out of the car, Niamh couldn't believe it, her mam looked positively radiant she was glowing like she had never seen her before.

'Mam, you look fantastic, whatever has happened to you these past few days, has certainly done the trick, wow mam, seriously, you look so radiant'

'I have been transformed into a woman with a mission'

'Oh, right oh, what is that then mam?'

'Let's get inside and get that kettle on and I will tell you about it pet'

Niamh couldn't wait to hear all of it, she listened with amazement and awe of her mam. My mam, she is a force to be reckoned with.

'I know there is a small adult teaching centre, just on the slope 100 yards from our Emily's shops mam, it looks like it has been refurbished. I only saw it the other week when Jack and I took a long walk'

'Oh! You and Jack, oh my pet, I am so happy to hear that news' as she hugged her daughter tightly.

'Don't get carried away mam, we are just dating, just dating, right'

'Right oh lass, I hear you'

Jacqueline had other ideas she liked Jack, he reminded her a little of Colm, steadfast and dependable.

The whole family arrived that night as Niamh called everyone around, they sat outside on this lovely June night and everyone brought snacks and drinks, it was a do-it-yourself night. Even Serena ventured out with Dylan. Jacqueline brought out the pouffe for Serena to rest her swollen ankles on.

Emily and Frankie shared out the snacks and drinks and the conversation flowed from the birth of the twins to the extension of the Emily shops, and then onto Jacqueline and her new venture into teaching.

Colm and Bernadette were quite happy huddled up in the corner of the garden listening on to the exciting conversation, they were too laid back to participate, as they were enjoying the glorious sand and rocky verges as they looked out at the sea.

As the night sky hovered over them it was time to call it a night. Niamh decided not to let on about the downfall of the Professor, it had been a glorious day, and it ended so brightly. Niamh wasn't going to dim this light, not today…

Chapter 26

The Summer was ending slowly, as the sun still beat a happy tune when it made its appearance.

Serena shuffled into the garden with her heavy weights on board, her stomach was no longer a small bump but a rather significant large bump, as she happily stroked her stomach, talking away to her two babies inside her.

'I do hope you are healthy in there as I have been very good and fed you well', as she talked away to herself.

The sun gleamed across the flower beds, she sat awhile and caught her breath. As soon as she was seated the backdoor gate opened and in walked Jacqueline for a visit.

'How lovely to see you Jacqueline, how are you?', Serena was puzzled as why Jacqueline had called so early and so soon?

'I just wanted to see how you were after having such an eventful night at the cottage last night. I hope it didn't wear you out too much'. Jacqueline really wanted to say that she hoped Serena still thought of her as reputable. She was aware that Serena and Dylan knew about the unfortunate liaison between her and the Professor, as she overhead Niamh on the telephone before their little gathering at the cottage.

There was a paused silence and Jacqueline moved towards Serena and blurted it all out.

'Oh! Serena, I do hope you still think of me as a good mother and person after my silly episode with the Professor, I am a little embarrassed and ashamed of my behaviour, although nothing happened between us'

Serena, bent towards Jacqueline as far as she could, her stomach seemed to have other ideas.

'Oh! please Jacqueline would you come closer, I cannot move forward, as you can see'.

They both laughed out loud, and Jacqueline moved her garden chair around.

'I am so proud of what you achieved Jacqueline, and as for the Professor, it was he who behaved badly and now he has been ostracized. He was lucky not to have gone to prison'

'What! I didn't know! Why didn't he go to prison, I heard he had intimate relations with several students. Did one of them complain to the Police?

'It turned out that Cheryl had made a bargain with the Professor by way of reimbursement of a substantial nature. I think it was around £1,000.00'

'My oh My, I knew that girl had a lot of gumption, but this, my what a triumph for her. She wasn't one for morals'

'How do you feel Jacqueline, really?'

'I think going on the retreat saved me in lots of ways Serena, if it hadn't been for Father Donnelly I think I may have lost myself completely'

'I am so happy you are back to your old self and now you can plan for the future, what do you think you will do now?'

'I am off to see the Principal of the Adult Centre just around the corner from Emily's shops in an hour', said Jacqueline.

Serena began saying,

'How exciting for you Jaqueline, that is great news, are you thinking of teaching there?

'Yes, I cannot wait to be honest, I am so looking forward to my interview. I must dash; it was lovely to see you"

Jacqueline departed and walked along the Coast Road; she didn't want to get the bus too early, so she walked to the next stop as it was a five-minute walk along the road.

Her thoughts drifted in and out, as she couldn't shrug off her conversation with Serena.

'Why am I thinking of that stupid man, he fooled me so. I must get rid of such stupid thoughts, and I will get rid of them'

She began thinking of what it would be like to be a teacher and help others; a sense of confidence and glow was upon her as he had the passion for learning and how she loved her books and poetry.

'I shall be consumed with the world of literature and learning, and may my prayers be answered'

She hurried now, as she could see the bus in the distance, she shot her right arm out so as the bus driver could see that she was alerting him. The bus slowed down, and the conductor helped her abroad.

'You just made it lass, let me give you a hand'

'Thank you,' said Jacqueline.

The bus ride was only ten-minute journey. She slowly gathered herself once of the bus and walked upright into the historical building, it looked rather like a small castle in its surroundings. A small garden, neatly assembled with its wrought iron gates all around. A courtyard towards the double-barrelled door, that looked as if it had been built for battle.

Jacqueline paused, then pressed the unusual bell that embedded in the wall at the side of the door. It made a marching tune as if soldiers were about to appear.

The door opened and there stood a woman in a black dress with a white collar. Her hair was slightly grey and was mounted on her head like a small pyramid. She spoke with a Scottish accent and welcomed Jacqueline in.

The hallway was dark in image as the wooden floors and staircase were all dark mahogany. The large chandelier brought significant light into this majestic building.

Mrs Clarkson introduced herself.

'I am the Head teacher here, we have six staff members, and we are hoping to select a further staff member by the end of the week, as term time is not too far away, and the successful candidate would need to be prepped and ready to start'

Jacqueline was so impressed so far and was determined to make a good impression; she was elevated to a high level as she walked into the principal's office. Mrs Clarkson was to oversee the interview.

Mr Grayson, the Principal was a tall thin man, rather bald with a thin rounded glass on. He greeted Jacqueline and she took her seat

Jacqueline sat neatly in her navy-blue suit and avoided crossed legs or arms, she felt that it would indicate a casualness about her, and she didn't want to give that impression.

He began by going through her degree and was impressed by the content and the cover letter that accompanied it.

'I would like to start with the question of, what makes you a good candidate for this position, tell us about yourself and your ambitions'

Jacqueline straightened her back, and nothing would hold her back as she began slowly, she remembered not to talk quickly. She energetically relayed to Mr Grayson; the point of teaching adults who have not achieved is to bring out their true potential that was hidden for so many years. To do that you must highlight their strengths and weaknesses and draw out a teaching plan to accommodate each of their needs. I believe that every student has potential and it's our job to get them to reach their full potential.

Mr Grayson sat back and was amazed at how Jacqueline was driven with commitment and desire to succeed. In his eyes it was so commendable in a candidate. He had seen quite a few and Jacqueline was top of his list.

Mrs Clarkson had had the same sentiments; it reminded her of herself when she applied some twenty years ago.

It was decided that Mrs Clarkson would show Jacqueline to the classrooms, each classroom was made of twenty students, not a large group, it was purposeful as Mr Grayson felt that the class should not be overcrowded as some students would get missed in the crowd.

They spent a further hour with Jacqueline going through their syllabus and the term time curriculum.

At this point, Mr Grayson had already made up his mind as too had Mrs Clarkson. They took Jacqueline back to the office and declared that she was to be the next member of staff.

Jacqueline was elated but confused as she thought she would have to wait until the end of the week. It was pointed out to Jacqueline that she was a good fit in every way, and they were delighted to have her on board.

She would receive a letter of appointment in the post by the end of the week, together with a start date. This date would be two weeks before term started.

It was a dream, she slowly walked down the stairs, and out to the courtyard, she couldn't feel her feet, she felt she was floating, an excitable dizziness came upon her as she sat on the bench in the courtyard.

'What just happened in there, what did I say, what did I do, I cannot remember what I did' as she laughed at herself.

She ran out of the courtyard and along the coast road, turning up the slope and into Emily's Shop.

Belinda greeted her and explained that Emily was in the Haberdashery shop next door, as they had just had a big delivery. She took Jacqueline through the adjacent door that was connected to the Wool shop.

As Jacqueline made her way through Emily was busy checking off the stock; the shop had grown so quickly, it was full of art and design, not to mention all the buttons, threads, materials and ornaments. Emily wasn't kidding she does need an extension.

'Mam, what a surprise what are you doing here, I wasn't expecting you,' said Emily.

'I have just been for an interview at the Adult Learning Centre, just down the slope and around the corner. Guess What happened?'

'What Mam, just get it out, why don't you'.

'I got the job as Teacher, I cannot believe it, I am still pinching myself!'

'I can Mam, I can, I am so proud of you', as Emily grabs her mam with tears in her eyes and hugs her tightly.

'Does Niamh know yet?'

'No, she is going for her placement teaching in Durham this afternoon, she had to go for a preliminary meeting before she starts next month. We can have a meal out tonight,' said Jacqueline.

'That sounds great mam, I am sorry Frankie, and I won't be able to come along, I will be here late with this lot of stock! and Frankie has a late job on too. We are just going to grab a fish supper tonight'

'I will see if Colm wants to come along and my sisters if they are not busy'.

'Let's have a celebratory coffee and cake in the meantime mam, I can have ten minutes off anyway', as Emily grabbed her purse and ushered her mam towards the café up the road.

They sat for more than ten minutes as Jacqueline was so animated she couldn't stop talking about the day. Emily was relieved and happy for her mam as she knew now, she had put the sleazy Professor behind her.

'I must get back mam, I have been away nearly an hour!'

'Oh! I am sorry pet, I have talked for England, it was lovely to catch up with you my pet'

'You can come for tea on Friday mam, we can talk some more, lots to talk about'

'I look forward to it pet', as Jacqueline kissed her daughter goodbye.

As she walked along the high street, she didn't want to go home and browsed among the shops, there was lovely dress shop on the corner, and she decided she would treat herself. There was a lovely autumn coloured dress in the window, it glowed, it beckoned her towards it.

'That would be a lovely dress for my first day at school, it would match the autumn leaves on the trees that would be coming out soon...' she thought to herself.

She entered the quaint little dress shop, as she opened the door a little bell rang. The shop assistant greeted her and guided her to rail in question and it was fortunate her size was there. A size 10, to fit Jacqueline's petite figure.

She went into the dressing room and looked at herself in the mirror and was amazed at what looked back at her.

'Is this really me, the new me, I quite like the new me'

The dress wasn't cheap it was two pounds! Her navy suit only cost one pound and half a crown. She was feeling too excited and waived the expense goodbye and bought it.

Just as she was leaving the shop, the bell rang and the door opened and in walked Cheryl, she didn't know Jacqueline, but Jacqueline knew her. She had ordered an expensive dress and was picking it up.

Jacqueline, stood outside for a moment and couldn't help but smile as she glanced towards the window.

'Yes, that girl knows what she wants, and it's called money'

Jacqueline was still smiling at herself as she made her way to the bus stop.

A new journey had begun she could feel it, and she embraced it with all her heart…

Chapter 27

The Autumn leaves scatter along the pathways, as the sun sets the trees alive with colour. It's that time of the year to savour. How the seasons transport us; Autumn with its cosy effect of a coal fire burning in the background.

Colm was first up on this cold morning in November, he had taken his dad's place on getting the coal fire prepared. He ran outside to collect the logs which were stored next to the coal bunker. He had his buckets ready, he was well drilled on this subject, as he loved to make the fire with his dad. He stood a moment and felt that whisper of wind on his back. For a moment he thought it was a hand, his dad's hand as he turned around with a hopeful look on his face.

'Nah! Get hold of yourself man, it's the wind, it's just the wind'

He gathered wood in one bucket and coal in the other. The newspapers were all piled up on the stool next to the fire and it didn't take long for Colm to have a roaring fire going. He sat back on the stool and reminisced for a while; his thoughts flashed back to that day when he and his dad were building the fire and his dad took his eye off the fire as the newspaper caught fire, what a morning that was. Declan had burned the rug, and Jacqueline was none too pleased. He got out the scrubbing brush and brushed away in the hope that he could salvage the carpet, he was making it worse. They all ended up laughing about it.

Colm's tears began to flow, he couldn't hold them back... Niamh entered the room and gave Colm a caring look.

'Hey bro, what's up? You ok, has something happened?'

'Nah! Just me reminiscing about dad, it caught me by surprise Niamh, I hadn't thought about him for ages'

Niamh sat on the floor next to Colm.

'It's does bro, it does, it happened to me the other week, when I was in the library. The memory of dad going through the history books and being so excited about what he had discovered. I think it's good for the soul to remember' as Niamh got up to make a cuppa.

Colm sat feeling the glow of the fire burning away. He looked at the clock and jumped up.

'Oh My! I just remembered I said I would go in early as new apprentices are starting, just time to sip that cuppa and I am off', as Colm ran up the stairs and into the bathroom.

Jacqueline came out of her bedroom.

'What is all this commotion about out here; you like school kids all over again!'

'I am late mam, said I would go in early, sorry for the clatter' as Colm brushed passed his mam. He was in a hurry alright as he grabbed a biscuit jumped into this car. He could hear his mam shouting out of the window

'Drive carefully, better to be safe than sorry'

Colm shouted back to his mam.

'Aye Mam aye, I hear you'

He drove along the coast road whistling away, he was looking forward to his new managerial role, as he was to train the new apprentices. The roads were busy and as he turned around the bend an MG car took the bend far too fast and smashed into Colm car, a Hillman Imp. Colm was dragged across the reservation and his car overturned and crashed into the shelter on the sea front.

Colm's face was smashed against the dashboard, he was bleeding heavily and lost consciousness. The man in the Jaguar wasn't hurt, he was distraught and ran to the nearby telephone box which was on the corner and dialled the emergency services. The Fire Brigade were alerted to a man trapped in his car.

The police arrived to restore some order with the pile of cars on the coast road. The Fire Brigade and Ambulance arrived within minutes. They prised the door off, and the paramedics took over. Colm had a week pulse, but he was alive, although unconsciousness. They had to act quickly, and they efficiently got him into the ambulance.

The Police took statements from the driver, and witnesses who saw the accident. It was evident that the driver was at fault, and he was taken to the police station for a further questioning. He was well dressed businessman and was reluctant to cooperate at first as he felt he had done nothing wrong. The three witnesses who saw the accident gave a concise statement of the situation.

A heated argument broke out as the driver was adamant he was in the right. The Policeman read him his rights and notified the driver that he would be charged with reckless driving, without due care or attention. The two Police man at the scene, escorted the driver to their police car and firmly put him in the back seat handcuffed as he resisted arrest.

The Ambulance arrived at the hospital and Colm was taking to the Emergency department, where he underwent a thorough examination. It was determined that he would need an x ray and scan on his chest and head. His chest was badly bruised, and his head had a big gash on the upper part of his forehead.

The Surgeon, Mr Charleston abruptly shouted to his team!

'Get that x ray over here now, let's see what we are dealing with!'

The x ray showed a contusion and swelling on the brain. Colm was quickly taken into theatre to be operated on.

Police Constable Jackson arrived at the Gibson's house and Jacqueline opened the door, with a frightened look on her face.

'What it is Constable, what is it'

'Let's go inside madame'

'No, I won't go inside, I won't go, tell me now, tell me here!'

'It's your son Colm; he has been in an accident'

Jacqueline cried out!

'He is alive please tell me he is alive!'

'He is at the Tyneside Hospital, that's all I know at the moment'

Jacqueline grabbed her coat and bag and followed the Constable out the door.

Niamh had left for work; she would call her later. She was in no mood to talk to anyone, she just wanted to get to the hospital to see her son.

As they arrived Jacqueline was informed that Colm was being operated on, and she must take a seat in the waiting room. She sat in the waiting room and began to think history was repeating itself.

'This cannot happen, please God' as she stroked the cross of our Lord that hung around her neck.

The Matron came into the room and asked Jaqueline if she wanted her to call anyone. Jacqueline mentioned her sister Sara who was working on one of the wards, she wasn't sure which one. The Matron gave a warm smile back at Jacqueline and spoke.

'Not to worry, I am sure we can track her down, leave it with me' as she patted Jacqueline on the shoulder.

Sara arrived half an hour later she quickly put her arms around Jacquline and said,

'Colm is strong our Jacqueline, he will get through this. I must telephone Bernadette; she needs to be here'

Jacqueline looked distraught as she turned to Sara

'Oh! I never thought, Bernadette, how selfish of me, I never thought'

Sara replied with a calmed response,

'It's alright Jacqueline, you were just thinking of your son, I will call her now, do you know her number?'

Jacqueline was good with telephone numbers but couldn't think for a moment.

'Just give me a minute, I know the number, yes, it's 629135, she might be the museum'

Sara rang the number and Bernadette's mam answered

'Oh no! Bernadette is working at the Branston Museum today, I have the number. I will call her'

After hearing the news, Bernadette quickly left the Museum and headed to the hospital she was holding herself together, as she wanted to drive in a calm state.

'I am not going to get upset, he will be alright, I must get there' as she muttered all the way to the hospital to herself.

The waiting room door opened, and Sara and Jacqueline gasped for a moment; it was Bernadette her eyes full of tears now, as she sees Sara and Jacqueline standing there.

They both comforted her and explained about the surgery. They were all told it would take up to three hours at least.

Sara went to get them all a strong cup of coffee. Jacqueline held Bernadette's hand, and they talked and talked about how Colm was excited about being a Manager in the Drawing Office, like his dad. They both decided he would be alright; he is a fighter.

Mr Charleston entered the room and took a step back for a moment, he was stunned, he hadn't realised Colm was Jacqueline's son. It had registered with him now; he had treated Declan.

Jacqueline spoke first

'Mr Charleston, it's you, Hello, you treated my late husband'

Mr Charleston look so surprised, and replied

'Colm has a contusion on the brain, they are no significant swellings and there is no excess fluid flowing around the brain. He has had a nasty contusion, and there is bruising on his chest which isn't severe. I am sure he will make a full recovery.

'Can I see him' Jacqueline with her pleading look at Mr Charleston.

'I am afraid not just yet, give a few hours for him to come around from the anaesthetic; I will take you along myself. You just take it easy and have a coffee and relax' as he smiled back at Jacqueline.

Sara looked across at Jacqueline as he left the room.

'Wow! Isn't he dishy, no wedding band either'

'What are you saying! our Sara, he was lovely to Declan'

'I think he has a twinkle in his eye when it comes to you dear sister' Sara smirks with a wry smile at Jacqueline.

Bernadette sat relieved with joy and joined in with the conversation and added

'I think he is dishy too, and he is coming back to take you along to see Colm'

'You are all coming along, what you mean, I don't know what you are talking about' as Jacqueline was confused, she had never thought of Mr Charleston like that he was her Declan's surgeon. She had never noticed any such admiration for her in the past.

Mr Charleston had a spring in his step as he strutted along the corridor; he was admired for his professionalism and most of the staff put up with his abruptness at times as they all knew he cared about his patients and showed it.

At this point he was hiding his emotions, he was in a turmoil, and he knew it. He quickly diverted into Colm's room to check everything was alright before gathering the family together.

As he entered the bedside and checked Colm chart and his vitals, he began waking up from the anaesthetic.

Colm mumbled away, 'Where I am, what's happening, why am I lying down'. He started to recover and then he remembered the bang.

Mr Charleston reassured him and gave him a full run down of what had occurred. Colm was amazed. All he could remember was being in the car and bang. He was told that he may have a short-term memory loss, but it shouldn't concern him too much. Mr Charleston was confident that Colm would fully recover from his nasty ordeal.

'You look familiar, are you the surgeon that treated my dad' as Colm looked at him curiously.

'I certainly am young man, and you are going to be fine lad, head like concrete I would say' as Mr Charleston made a candid gesture to break the ice.

Colm smiled back at him and replied.

'My mam would agree with you on that one'

'Talking of your mam, she is waiting down the corridor with your girlfriend and Auntie. They are eagerly waiting to see you. I will go and fetch them'

Colm felt the pain all over his body, but he was alive, and he was grateful for that.

As Mr Charleston walked steadily along corridor, his thoughts turned to Jacqueline

'Maybe I should ask Jacqueline out for coffee, or should I say lunch'

He opened the waiting room door and looked straight into Jacqueline's eyes, with a loving look… Sara and Bernadette looked at each other thinking the same thing.

'Oh! Mr Charleston has that look, that look of love.

Sara and Bernadette dragged behind a little so that Mr Charleston and Jacqueline could walk along together.

As he turned his head to speak to all of them, he explained that Colm was awake, and he was going to make a full recovery.

'However, ladies, we will keep him here for a week just to get him up and about as he has been banged about quite a bit. I don't want him overdoing it not just yet'

They all entered the room. Jacqueline kissed her son and held his hand for a moment and said she would visit that very evening. It was decided after a few minutes that Colm and Bernadette have their personal time together as Mr Charleston escorted Jacqueline and Sara out.

Sara made her excuses as she had to get back on the ward and left Mr Charleston and Jacqueline to it.

He walked Jacqueline out.

'Can I see you to your car?' as he gave her a warm smile.

'I don't drive Mr Charleston; I get the bus'.

He was taken back and quickly responded by saying,

'If you give me five minutes, I will drive you home, it's my lunchtime anyway'

Jacqueline was so surprised; she wasn't expecting such a gesture of goodwill.

'Thank you, I will wait over here', as she made her way to the golden auburn tree, that shone a golden shadow across the pathway. There was a quaint little bench at the side of the glorious tree.

Mr Charleston looked back at Jacqueline sitting under the tree, and muttered to himself

'What a vision of loveliness' as hurriedly went to his office to retrieve his jacket and keys.

As he made his way back to Jacqueline, he escorted her to his car a beige/pastel green Plymouth roadrunner, a robust car. He loved his car, as there was plenty of room for his big labrador dog, Jasper. A lovely brown labrador with his shiny coat. His sister Clarissa looked after Jasper when he was working, as he didn't like leaving him alone.

Jacqueline commented on his robust car, and the conversation began about his dog Jasper. He talked about his farmhouse dwelling. His late father was a farmer and farmed the land. Mr Charleston sold the land and stock of cows to the nearby farmer as he was no farmer, but he loved the farmhouse and renovated it to his taste. He did have a stable annexed for his horses, three of them. Daisy, Thunderbolt, and Jester. Thunderbolt was his horse a large horse with a shiny brown coat.

As the conversation flowed, he turned to Jacqueline and spoke

'Please call me Jason, Mr Charleston sounds so formal, keep that for the hospital'

They had arrived at Jacqueline's cottage and Jacqueline thanked Jason. He couldn't hold back and just came out with it.

'Jacqueline, would you like to go to dinner one night, and we can talk some more about you and what you like to do. I seem to have talked your head off all the way home'

Jacqueline smiled back at him and replied

'Yes, that would be lovely'

He eagerly replied

'How about Saturday evening, I will pick you up at 7pm, that is to say, if I don't see you before at the hospital'

As she opened her front door and turned around to wave goodbye to Jason, her thoughts strayed towards Declan once again; a look of dismay hit her when she shut the door.

'What the hell just happened; I am confused, yes, the girls said it, he is rather dishy. but I am not ready for such another encounter with an attractive man. I will tell him no when I see Colm tomorrow.

'Another episode in my life, I keep having them, as she sat with a cup of tea and pondered…about the whole thing. Another day, another episode…

Chapter 28

Niamh arrived home from her busy day teaching in Durham. She was finding it a little hard with the Year 11 as they had strong opinions about everything. The Head of year assured Niamh that when she had finished her placement, she would have more confidence. He was impressed with her work ethic and gave her a lot of encouragement to carry on. She was going to stay as she loved teaching some much. It was exhausting at times, but nevertheless truly rewarding.

As she put the key in the door, she was notified about Colm and his accident. The whole day went out of her head as she grabbed her keys and made her way to the hospital before Jacqueline had finished telling her all about the day's events.

Niamh was anxious as she drove, she and Colm were close and the effects of losing her dad seem to take over her thoughts once again.

She arrived and briskly marched into the hospital towards Colm's ward. He was sitting up with his head bandaged reading one of his football magazines, no doubt it was Newcastle United.

As he looked up, he gave a wry smile,

'What's up sis, what do you know', he cheekily winked at Niamh.

'What's up, I'll tell you what's up; my heart was in my mouth when mam told me. I didn't stop to listen to the rest of the conversation, I just dashed over as quickly as I can. I thought you would be out for the count' as she gave out a rather nervous laugh. It sounded more like a cry.

'Come sit by me sis, I am alright sis, as he held her hand. I am coming home in a few days; they are just observing as it's a head injury. I feel fine really, I do'

'Mr Charleston the surgeon is looking after me, you know, the one that looked after dad'.

Niamh looked stunned and replied with sad look on her face.,

'Oh, I see, I am so happy you are alright. I bet Bernadette was upset with all of this?'

Colm looked down for a minute.

'She is alright now; she has been here since I had the accident. I sent her home for some rest. I said she could do with it'. As he grinned away.

'You would, you cheeky so and so' as Niamh grabbed his hand.

Mr Charleston arrived in the room and made his presence known as he stood at the bottom of the bed and informed Colm; he could go home the next day as his bloods, and cognitive measures of balance when walking were fine.

As Mr Charleston turned to Niamh.

'It is nice to see you again, I may see you on Saturday when I pick your mam up for dinner', he spoke with such an eager response.

This response unsettled Niamh a little, she was more than unsettled, she was flabbergasted at such a notion. All she could respond with was

'Oh, I see', with an utterly confused look on her face.

He left Niamh and Colm to talk on their own.

'Did you know about this our Colm? As she shouted over the bed.

'No, I didn't, he is a nice guy, don't you think?

Niamh's eyes began to spread widely,

'He might be a nice guy, but this is our mam, and she has been through a lot lately. She must have said yes, as he seems so sure of it'.

Niamh kissed her brother goodbye and said she would pick him up tomorrow to take him home.

She drove home rather speedily, as she wanted to find out more about what had happened between her mam and Mr Charleston.

She entered the kitchen to find her mam washing up.

'Mam, what is this about Mr Charleston and you going out to dinner. I have just spoken to him at the hospital. His face lit up like a Christmas Tree when he said he was taking you to dinner'

Jacqueline sat down and at that moment and spoke in a cool manner,

'It's only dinner pet; I don't think for a moment anything will come of it'. Jacqueline at this point was trying hard to convince herself of this. She had enjoyed the car drive home with him. He made good conversation about nature and what it was like being brought up on a farm. She was interested in what he had to say.

Niamh sat her weary legs down and the subject was changed to her day at the school.

'You will be an excellent teacher pet, you will; you just listen to the head', Jacqueline got up and put her arm around Niamh's shoulders.

They both heard a loud knock at the door,

'Who can that be, they certainly know how to use the knocker!' Niamh shouted as she made her way to the door,

'I am coming! I am coming! Hold your horses why don't you!

It was Dylan and Emily hoping for news about Colm.

'Well, hello you two, some knock that was Uncle Dylan, mam jumped out of her skin!' as Niamh winked at her uncle Dylan.

'Sorry about that, I hadn't realised I hit it so hard, how's Colm doing, we are heading over to the hospital in a bit?' as Dylan sheepishly walked past Niamh.

Niamh explained to her Uncle Dylan and Emily that Colm was doing great, and he will be home tomorrow, earlier than expected.

Dylan quickly jumped in

'I wouldn't expect anything less for Colm, he doesn't like hospitals at the best of times,'

Niamh said that she had some more news that might shock them both.

'Mam is going out to dinner with Mr Charleston on Saturday night'

Dylan smiled and put his arm around this sister-in-law

'He is a nice guy our Jacques, you should go and enjoy yourself'.

Emily however, looked a little surprised as she looked at Niamh. Niamh gave her hand sign to follow her into the hall.

'What is it our Niamh?'

'I don't think it's a good idea; mam has just come out of a terrible ordeal with the professor' Niamh pulled Emily's arm away from the door carried on with the conversation.

'What do you think our Emily?'

Emily looked confused

'I don't know, maybe it might be a happy distraction for mam; he was lovely when he looked after dad'

They both made their way back into the kitchen and joined in the conversation that had turned to Serena and the twins. Dylan was telling Jacqueline that she was getting so big now and her back was giving her a lot of pain.

'I oversee the daily leg, and ankle rubs and several back rubs every day. She cannot wait to give birth now. It's six to eight weeks away. She is loving her cross stitch more that the knitting, but she has knitted quite a lot of bootees and lovely cross stitch portraits these passed weeks. It has kept her busy'

Emily was delighted at the news and said she would accompany Dylan back to his house to visit Serena.

Dylan was pleased with Emily's suggestion.

'Serena will be made up Emily. She will want to show off her new creations'

Serena was seated at the dining room table when Dyland and Emily arrived, and she had a look of joy when she got a glimpse of Emily behind Dylan.

'Oh, Emily it is so good to see you, I am just sorting out some frames for my cross-stitch portraits' as she gathered her things together.

Emily was taken back by the great craftsmanship that Serena had produced and commented on all of them. She pointed out that they wouldn't look out of place in the haberdashery shop, or even the new art shop she was developing now.

The contracts were exchanged, and the Art shop would be a great addition to the wool shop and haberdashery shop, as Emily had so much artwork stored, it wouldn't be long before the art shop was full of beautiful paintings.

Serena was over the moon to hear such lovely comments from Emily, and they sat together and went through all Serena's works and there quite a few. Her knitting however, consisted of two pairs of mittens and two hats. Serena had taken to the cross-stitch so much as she had created landscapes and beautiful flower arrangements. It was all so impressive.

Emily looked over them once again and couldn't believe how Serena had become so proficient at this; it was only a month ago that she had started her first lesson of knitting and cross-stitch.

She turned to Serena with a complimentary smile on her face.

'You do realise that some people take months and months to prefect such remarkable portraits as these. I am putting these in the shop'

Serena got up to sit on the chair and Dylan gathered her footrest and placed her swollen ankles onto it. She instructed Dylan to get the kettle on and get the ginger cake out which her mam had left earlier that day.

They all sat and talked away about the babies and Dylan gave Emily a tour upstairs to the nursery when she had finished her tea.

She loved the neutral colour of the pale yellow as they had no idea if the twins were boys or girls, they could add some more colour when they were born. The nursery was so beautifully assembled with the lace curtain draped upon the cots.

Serena's mam being a painter had completed the walls with a rainbow and added some sparkle with a lovely delicate sky above; this highlighted the lovely pale-yellow background. It looked so bright and cheerful.

Emily looked up at Dylan

'You look a little tired Uncle, you should take some rest, you are going to need it when the babies come along'

Dylan shook his head,

'Nah! It's happy tired, I will be fine, stamina of an ox me '.

Emily with a non-convincing look on her face

'No man is an ox; you look after yourself mind' as she waved her finger at him.

They made their way downstairs, and Emily said Goodbye to them. She wanted to get home to Frankie to tell him that the art shop would be finalised next week, and the shop would be open for business just in time for Christmas, which was only five weeks away…

Frankie was already home, and he had in fact got the table ready for tea. Emily walked in the kitchen with a curious look on her face,

'What is this then? A table already for tea, but have you put the chops in the oven my pet, I think maybe that is too much a tall order don't know, I will have to teach you how to turn the oven on'. Emily had spotted the chops on top of the oven in a tray, in readiness for cooking, presumably by Emily's fair hands. They both looked at one another and Frankie smirked at his wife,

'Nah, you are alright pet, I will leave the cooking to you, we wouldn't want the house burning down now would we'

They both sat at the table with a cup tea while the chops, potatoes vegetables were cooking away.

Frankie began with a little concern on his face

'Are you sure pet about this art shop, do not think the two shops you already have are enough pet?'

Emily jumped up and retaliated with a spring in her step as she stirred the vegetables in the pan,

'I do not love; I have everything planned. Charlotte, Serena's mam is on board, she will be doing some portraits for us, as you know she is a lovely painter. I have organised interviews for next week for assistants and a supervisor, everything will work like clockwork. Uncle Arthur has supplied me with a good accountant for the bookkeeping. We will be fine love. It's always been my dream to have three shops co-ordinating with each other. I couldn't be happier love'

Frankie was astonished, he couldn't believe it as he gave his wife a look of pride.

'You are amazing, you really are, I don't' know how you do it'

'It's called just getting organised before the event my love', Emily put her arm around Frankie and kissed his head. She made her way to the stove and all the food was cooked and ready to serve.

After tea they made their way into the sitting room and talked about Colm and the accident.

He was happy to retrieve the car from the accident and take it to the garage and fix the front and side panel of the car. The damage to the car wasn't that bad at all as envisaged. Emily said she would pay for the damage as Colm and Bernadette were saving up for their first holiday together after Christmas.

They sat by the roaring fire, on the settee. Emily placed her head on Frankie's chest, and he looked down at his wife's lovely face and kissed her forehead.

'I love these autumn evenings by the fireside. We will have to think about a Christmas Tree soon and decorations. Let's have the Tree in that corner so we can admire it from here what you think my pet?' as he lifted Emily's head up.

'Mmm she spoke, I think just a little to the left maybe, it will have a more focal point, it will light up better from here', as Emily made her way to the corner.

Frankie smiled at his wife,

'Yes, you are the architect my pet, you know where things need to be'

They hugged in a passionate embrace.

'Early night pet' as Frankie winked at his wife

'Yes, my love, I think so '

They both held hands and ran upstairs laughing away to the bedroom and slammed the door behind them... ....

Chapter 29

Jason Charleston awoke at 6am, turning his head, his eyes not quite opened as he could hear the alarm from the clock with its incessant ring! He lunged over the bed with his right arm and pressed the alarm button off so firmly, the clock tilted and fell off the bedside cabinet! He got out of bed grunting away and made his way to the bathroom. He was washed and dressed so efficiently; his impeccable routine never failed him.

He made his way downstairs and looked around his living room, this quaint old style farmhouse cottage. He hadn't done a lot of work to it as he was too busy at the hospital. He stood in the middle of the room with his hands on his head muttering away to himself...

'Well, it has character, at least. It just needs a woman's touch'. The wood beamed ceiling looked magnificent. He despaired at the lack of light in the room as it was rather cluttered. He decided to remove some of the furniture and pull the drapes right back.

'That looks much better' as he stroked his chin to assure himself it did.

His housekeeper who cleaned once a week was not due for a few more days, he would try and persuade to come along today being Friday. He was hoping Jacqueline would like to visit. His plan was to call her and invite her around on Saturday afternoon and they could go out to dinner afterwards.

First things first, let's call her first to see if she would agree. The telephone rang out for a few minutes, and he was just about to hang up then Jacqueline answered it.

'Hello'

Mr Charleston paused?

'Hello, is anyone there'

He took a deep breath and replied energetically

'Hello, Jacqueline, its Jason here. I am calling to ask if you would like to visit my humble abode tomorrow afternoon. I could give you a tour of the place and introduce to my horses. He could then go to the restaurant for dinner at 7pm'

It was Jacqueline's turn to pause a moment, she took several moments.

Mr Charleston was getting a little nervous at this point.

'Hello! Are you still there?' said he

Jacqueline quickly answered

'Yes, I am still here, and yes, shall we say 2pm tomorrow', she couldn't believe what she had just said, as she put her hand over mouth in amazement.

Mr Charleston leaned back from the telephone with an enormous smile on his face and answered with a soft tone to his voice.

'We shall have a lovely afternoon; we can take a nice stroll across the hilltop. Bring some walking shoes with you'

As they both put the phone down. Mr Charleston quickly picked it up to call his housekeeper Mrs Biggins. She was happy to do a few hours cleaning as Mr Charleston had offered twice the amount of her original pay being one pound.

Jacqueline was in a frenzy; she had just realised that she would need two outfits.

'There is only one solution to this dilemma, I will have to change at his house for dinner' said she with an anxious look on her face.

She made her way to the wardrobe and pulled her some slacks and striped shirt, and her walking boots she wore when walking along the beach.

'That will do for the daytime, that is sorted' said she, not convincingly.

'My navy-blue dress with white daisies on and my navy-blue shoes', that's it, no more to be said, as she sat on the end of the bed and caught herself in the mirror.

'Am I kidding myself or am I going to have a little adventure. Oh, I need an adventure Declan', as she looked at his picture next to her bed. She kissed the photograph and made her way downstairs.

Jacqueline headed to her classroom at the Adult Centre; she entered the classroom bright and breezy, her mannerism seemed to uplift the whole of the class today and she was animated like she had never been before.

At the end of class some of the students went up to Jacqueline and thanked her for the most vibrant lesson of poetry. Some students had said they had been converted. The room was buzzing with enthusiasm. The school day had ended with smiles all around the classroom.

Jacqueline left the school building that day at 4pm with a sudden urge to skip all the way home, but she held herself back, as she remembered where she was in the street, and the best way forward was to take the bus home in an orderly manner as she grinned all the way home.

As she took in the sights along the coast road, it was a drizzly day, that didn't matter to Jacqueline, it was sun shining in her mind. There were still lots of dog walkers out with their dogs, as she watched the world go by through the bus window, she felt herself humming and looked at the person next to her; a woman with a checked headscarf on who was giving her a look of wonder?' She probably thinks I am mad', as Jacqueline smiled at her. The lady moved seats as she was not quite sure of the person next to her on the bus...

Jacqueline quickly got up as her stop was upon her. She now wanted to skip her way to her front door, and she did so hum, hum, she did, all the way...

She hadn't noticed Niamh coming through the front gate.

'Mam are you alright, I have never seen you like this, I just caught you skipping mam as I got out of the car, have we won the football pools this week?'.

Jacqueline turned to Niamh with a caring eye,

'No pet, I have had a fabulous day with my students, and they loved it, it was extraordinary to hear Bill Baggaley say he now likes poetry it's a revelation, it truly is'

Niamh eyes widened with such love in them,

'Oh, mam I am so happy for you, I really am'

They sat together on the settee and Jacqueline began to tell Niamh about the telephone conversation with Mr Charleston.

Niamh's expression dampened a little with that look of concern on her face.

Jacqueline stood up next to the fireplace,

'It's alright our Niamh, I am going to have a lovely afternoon out walking with Mr Charleston and have dinner, nothing more than that my pet, so don't concern yourself'

Niamh tentatively looked on and turned her face away from her mam for moment and then responded with a light-hearted approach

'The weather forecast is rather good tomorrow, Jack and I are going to the promenade as there is a band performing after the crafts fair which starts at 2pm, well mam, you should have a lovely day walking mam'

They both got up and hugged each other.

Niamh suggested they go out for a celebratory drink. Afterall the week had been a great success.

'Let's leave Colm a note to meet us at the bistro,' said Niamh.

Colm turned up with Bernadette, as Colm had some news for them both. Before he could tell them the news, Niamh immediately spotted a diamond ring on Bernadette's third finger left hand.

'Oh, my goodness, you are engaged, look mam, they are engaged' Niamh grabbed hold of Bernadettes hand with such joy on her face, 'It's about time, how did this happen, tell us everything'

Jacqueline grabbed her son's face and kissed his cheek lovingly and responded

'I knew he would make an honest woman of you Bernadette',

Bernadette began saying that she was more surprised than anyone, it had just happened an hour ago. Colm butted in...

'I have been preparing for this for a month! The only person who knew was Uncle Dylan and even he was getting agitated with me. I was saving up for the right ring, I wanted the one Bernadette loved. I went about the deception rather cunningly', as Colm winked at Bernadette.

'How did you manage that bro', said Niamh curiously.

'Well, I took Bernadette to the jewellers and pretended I was looking for a ring for mam for her Christmas present. I got Bernadette to look at all the diamond rings and when she picked out the small cluster of diamonds in the dress ring section. I noticed a cluster of diamonds in the engagement ring section which were almost identical. So, there you have it folks.

Bernadette was beaming with joy and agreed, the ring was just perfect.

Niamh stood up,

'Here is a toast to Colm and Bernadette, may your days be filled with love and happiness'

Everyone raised their glasses and spoke

'Amen to that'.

Bernadette was keen to get home and let her mam and brother know her good news.

Jacqueline stood up and looked towards Colm,

'I wish dad was alive to see this day',

They all looked at one another and Colm glanced at his mam, thinking the same thing she was, if only dad was here too. He knew that look and Niamh too looked towards her mam.

Jacqueline went on to say, that it had been the most marvellous day all round and want a lovely surprise you two, you have made my day so perfect. Thank you, off you go to Bernadette's give my love to her mam.

Niamh and Jacqueline sat awhile and reminisced about the past.

'I think dad would have loved Bernadette, she is so right for Colm, they are so well suited so laid back'. said Niamh.

Jacqueline didn't answer straight away as she was thinking more of what was to happen the next day with Mr Charleston. Her mood had dipped; those feelings of joy had disappeared… Bernadette had brought her back down to earth with the thoughts of her late father. She started having doubts once again about meeting Mr Charleston.

'Mam, where are you, where did you just go? Don't dwell mam, Dad wouldn't want you to dwell for this long mam, I know he wouldn't' as Niamh grabbed her mam's hand.

'My oh my, our Niamh, you have certainly changed your tune, I thought you didn't want me to go and meet Mr Charleston tomorrow?' said Jacqueline.

'I know, I know, I just cannot get over how happy you were this afternoon, and that makes me happy, it makes me very happy', so let's drink to that mam, happiness'.

The next day, Niamh was up early; the seagulls and birds made sure, they were in good song this morning. The sunshine had brought a loud array of promise, and the day looked so promising as Niamh opened her curtains to a blue sky and sun already set and burning brightly.

Jacqueline was bathed and dressed. She was already in the kitchen and Niamh could smell the bacon and eggs cooking; that aroma of smoky bacon which was more inviting to Colm as he shouted down from upstairs.

'I am a coming for that lovely breakfast mam, it smells delicious'

Niamh, however, was a corn flakes or toast person, she never liked a heavy breakfast.

They all sat around the breakfast table, talking away about their plans for the day. Colm was making his way to Bernadette's to take her mam out for lunch to celebrate. Niamh was being picked up. Jack would arrive at 10am. Jacqueline had the morning to contemplate her afternoon and evening out with Mr Charleston.

The time had come, and Mr Charleston entered the pathway of Jacqueline's cottage and rang the bell. He stood back combing his brown hair back, shaking a little. He wore a casual checked shirt with brown corduroy trousers and lumbar jack style jacket. Jacqueline had never seen him in this attire, he looked like a country man rather than a surgeon. She greeted him with a warm smile and invited him into the hallway.

'I am afraid I got a change of clothing to bring with me, as you did say we would be outdoors' said Jacqueline as she smiled at him. She had put her dress in an enclosed fabric protector and put her accessories in a small holdall.

Mr Charleston quickly grabbed Jacqueline things and put them in the car. Jacqueline followed him out directly.

They were off, and the conversation quickly turned the sun beaming away on this frosty December day. They talked of the Christmas period coming up in three weeks and they had noticed some people had their decorations already up. Jacqueline always put her decorations up 12 days before and took them down 12 days after. He was a spiritual thing with Jacqueline. The twelfth night; the epiphany., the manifestation of Jesus to the world, which is also known as the three kings' day.

Mr Charleston laughed as she drove through the coastline towards to his farmhouse cottage.

'I haven't really thought about Christmas yet, I am usually working, and most Christmas Days I have had a Christmas dinner in the hospital restaurant if I had the time that is' he said with a glum tone in his voice.

Jacqueline was shocked she had no idea; she assumed he would be home with family, a mother, or a sister. He went to his sisters on boxing day usually.

They arrived at his cottage and Jacqueline was pleasantly surprised at the humbleness of it, she imagined it to be a rather big place, but it was a quaint three bedroomed cottage, barnlike effect from the outside.

He showed Jacqueline the back room where she could change in, as it was the tidiest. His bedroom was always cluttered as he never really gave it much thought other than it was a place to sleep in.

Jacqueline laid her clothes on the Edwardian bed, which was another surprise, he delicate woodwork on the headboard took her attention. This is an expensive bed she thought to herself. She hung her dress on the wardrobe door as she pulled it ajar, so it would hang properly. The contents in the wardrobe were full of shirts and suits and trousers and a shoe rack with several pairs of men's brogue shoes.

She made her way downstairs, and Mr Charleston had a pot of coffee on the go, and they sat in the dining room, he had two large fireplaces, one in the living room and one in the dining room. He had them both lit. The rooms were cosy and warm.

'What do you think of the place, it's a little dated, but it's still having some unique features' said Mr Charleston with a pleading look on his face.

Jacqueline quickly responded with

'I think it is absolutely charming; it has the essence of a country farmhouse; you can almost imagine the taste the country food'.

'Well, you certainly have a vivid imagination Jacqueline,' as he smiled back at her.

It was time for their walk and Jacqueline was invigorated after their afternoon of walking. She was famished and ready for the dinner at restaurant. It was a country pub/bistro, the Pelican which was had the elegant feature of the Pelican illustrated on the wrought iron billboard hanging outside the pub.

The food was hearty, and Jacqueline was ready for her homemade mince and dumplings which was on the menu. She also enjoyed the jam Roly poly pudding. She didn't usually eat that much, but the long walk had given her an appetite.

Mr Charleston was impressed with Jacqueline's appetite and pointed it out so

'You have eaten your meal with such conviction, I love the way you tucked into your mince and dumplings with great intent' as she smiled with such admiration.

Jacqueline blushed a little and replied

'I don't usually feel this hungry, but it was delicious'.

As they made their way back to the cottage, Jacqueline began feeling a little uneasy and it wasn't long after that Mr Charleston made that important gesture.

'I will give you a minute to collect your things and I will run you home young lady and thank you for the most enjoyable day'.

Jacqueline sighed with joy, the joy of meeting a gentleman, she too commented on the day.

He saw Jacqueline to her door and kissed her softly and said goodnight, until he next time.

Jacqueline slowly entered her hallway and sat a moment, it had a wonderful day, she wanted to tell Declan, and she did so. At bedtime she sat with his picture and told him all about it and fell asleep with Declan's picture on her bed......

Chapter 30

It was beginning of December, and bitter wind would not be quietened. The glorious sun seemed to drown out the low temperatures as it beamed in and out of the sleety showers.

Colm was not deterred by this cold and brisky morning, he was still in his singing mode and was up and ready to start his day at work. His mind wasn't on work, he was too busy thinking about wedding plans for he and Bernadette couldn't make up their minds up whether to have a spring or summer wedding.

Jacqueline looked upon her dear son and couldn't believe how grown up he looked in his suit and tie, as he turned to her, she saw a glimpse of Declan in him and was pleased to see such a vision as Colm did have some of his dad's characteristics.

'See you later mam, must dash, lots to sort out, as we have a ship in dry dock this morning, and you know what that means, I will have to get cracking with the specifications and alterations. I love it when you start a new ship and draw out the new specifications…,' said Colm.

'You are just sounding like your dad dear lad, he would be so proud of you', said Jacqueline.

He waved goodbye and winked at his mam.

Jacqueline stood awhile and ruminated her thoughts towards the day and tasks in hand. It was a busy week at the adult centre as they break up for Christmas holidays, after all, it is only a few weeks away Christmas, so much to do, as she muttered to herself.

She gathered her satchel full of pupil's essays, she had marked them all and there were some very good compositions. Jacqueline had asked the pupils to write their own Christmas story based on their own experiences. She had noticed some pupils had quite a creative talent as some of them let their imagination run away with them.

It was of course Cara, she had written a story about air hostess trapped on a plane with aliens in a storm on Christmas Eve, it was quite inventive, and little far-fetched at times throughout the storyline. Jacqueline liked a creative mind and encouraged the students to come out of their comfort zone. It worked for some, and there were those who were hard work,

Niamh was ready to give her mam a lift to adult centre, as she too was having a busy week teaching. They swapped conversations about the end of term. Niamh had settled at her school teaching, and she was looking forward to a long career there now, she had got over her inhibitions.

'How is Jack pet, is he coming to us for Christmas, or are you going to his house, you haven't said much about Christmas festivities'?' as Jacqueline turned her head to Niamh hoping that she would say that she was staying at home and Jack was coming too.

Niamh began saying that she hadn't mentioned anything to Jack, but she would in due time...

'I have a lot on at school mam, as you know I have been roped into doing a Christmas play for year 11. It's called, 'The Christmas Holiday'. It is based around the 1940s, after the war. We have our rehearsals all week and the final show is on Friday the last day at school. I want all the family to attend mam', I know Serena won't be able to, but I hope Uncle Dylan will come along'

Jacqueline had no idea, she felt a little guilty, as her mind had been on another, namely, Mr Charleston. She felt terrible as she then recalled Niamh had mentioned it before, but it had not registered with her.

'Oh, that is fabulous pet, I knew you would do a great job, you are so creative pet. You are a good writer, I always thought you would go into journalism, but I am so happy that you have chosen teaching for you are so good at it my pet,' said Jacqueline.

Niamh was feeling a little guilty as she hadn't seen her uncle or Serena for some time,

'I will call Uncle Dylan later, I feel terrible I have not been around to see Serena lately, I keep on meaning to but there doesn't seem to be enough time, said she.

Jacqueline responded by saying,

'Our Emily has been spending a good deal of time with her as she has been collecting all Serena's cross stitch portraits for the gallery. She is going to display them all over the Christmas period. Serena has created a lovely Christmas portrait of a beautiful mantelpiece with a Christmas Tree by the side of it. I am looking forward to seeing it in the shop'.

Niamh was animated,

'Oh my! I am so pleased for Serena, she has really taken to this, a far cry from the legal system. I wonder if she will carry on with it after the twins are born?' said she.

'I do believe that she may have her hands full with the twins', as Jacqueline laughed out loud.

As the week progressed, Niamh was now ready for the big night. The play was ready to go live! All the pupils were in place ready for action...

Jack was in the front row with his mam and all he Gibson Family had arrived. Dylan had left Serena at home with her mam, as she was coming up to her due date, it could be in the next few weeks, or it could be sooner; you never know with babies...

As the curtains opened the scene was set. The pupils were dressed in their war time uniforms. It was a bar room setting, with a Christmas tree in the corner. The Glen Miller music started, and the pupils had learned their lines perfectly, and their steps for the dance routine. How they bopped around the floor with such vigour and enthusiasm.

The play was a great success. The audience stood up, what a standing ovation, it lasted for five minutes... Jack was filled with pride, as he looked on towards Niamh. He was so in love with her, but he still had doubts, his lack of courage prevented him from moving forward with the relationship, he always seemed to take a step back...

Jacqueline turned her head around and towards the back of the room was Mr Charleston, he had arrived late, but nevertheless he arrived... one of his operations had taken longer than anticipated.

He made his way towards Jacqueline, and she met him halfway...

'I am so sorry that I was a little late, I couldn't get away. As Jason whispered in Jacqueline's ear, this play looks marvellous, I love the theme of a Wartime Christmas... You cannot beat a bit of Glen Miller music can you' as he smiled down at Jacqueline'.

She was lost in his face for a moment and gathered herself.

'Yes, it was such a good play, and the pupils were so good, I am so proud of our Niamh'

They both made their way out to the car park.

Jason turned to Jacqueline and said,

'Are you free tomorrow, I was wondering if you would like to go to Christmas Fayre in the village just down the road from me, it's renowned for its excellent stalls and there is some entertainment on later, if you fancy that', as he willingly looked into Jacqueline eyes.

'Oh, tomorrow, well, yes, I would love to, what time?' Jacqueline looked a little astounded at her reply, she looked rather starry eyed.

'I will pick you up at 10.00am'.

Dylan, Frankie and Emily strolled passed them both and looked on with curiosity. Dylan was the first to start the conversation and asked Jacqueline if she needed a lift home. Jason butted in immediately, and said,

'I have got this Dylan; I can drive Jacqueline home'.

Dylan smiled at them both and as he walked away, he winked back at Jacqueline. Emily and Frankie said a quick hello and then goodbye as they walked alongside Dylan.

Emily turned to Dylan and said,

'What do you think Uncle Dylan, do you think there is anything in this friendship mam has with Mr Charleston'.

Dylan quickly replied,

'I think he has put some happiness back in Jacqueline's eyes, and for me, that is good thing'.

Emily seemed subdued about it all, but she was happy that her mam looked like she was having a nice time.

The nightfall came and as Jacqueline went to close her bedroom curtains, she felt an overwhelming warm come over her, it was the sight of that orange glowing sky that sat behind the clouds like sun beam mountains… It will be sunny tomorrow she thought as she slipped into her bed.

She awoke and could see the sun beaming through the curtain gap; it is going to be a lovely day at the Christmas Fayre, she beamed with joy.

Dylan, awoke as Serena poked him in the back, I think I have started!

'Started what my love?'

'I am in Labour, you fool, labour, oh! let's just see, it might be wind, let's give it a minute' as Serena stroked her tummy.

Half an hour later she shouted,

'Dylan this Is not wind, we need to go, have you got bag you packed last week'

Dylan in a flustered state,

'What bag'.

'Serena shouted, the bag! We need to go my love, now, not later now!

He Scrambled about, not in a good state.

Serena realised he was not going to be able to do this. She told him to ring Jacqueline, she is so sensible and calm, maybe her surgeon friend might come along, as Serena was a little frenzied at this time. The contractions were getting closer, too close for comfort...

Dylan's hand was shaking as he dialled Jacqueline's number, she was just about to head out the door, as Jason was in the hall and they were off to the Christmas Fayre, or so they thought...

Jacqueline picked up the receiver and said,

'Hello'

Dylan shouted down the telephone!

'Thank God you have picked up, can you come now! Serena is in labour, and I cannot find the packed bag! You are closer to us than anyone, and calmer! I don't know what to do!

Jacqueline calmly replied.

'Sit tight, we will be with you in five minutes'

Jacqueline explained to Jason, and he was more than happy to go along, although he had not trained for this, but he had a steady hand and a good bedside manner which was needed in this case,

Serena was frantic, puffing and blowing, Dylan was hopeless he had no idea what to do, he got a wet cloth and put it on Serena brow.

She snapped at him.

'Get it off me, get it off me, you silly man!

The doorbell rang and Dylan was happy to see them both. Jason hurried up the stairs and could see that Serena was further gone than he had anticipated. He quickly rang one of his colleagues, an obstetrician Mr Sanders, who thankfully answered the telephone. He was half an hour away, but things began to progress.

Jason went into surgeon mode and went to the bathroom, scrubbing his hands. He instructed Jacqueline to get plenty of towels.

He placed three pillows under Serena, got her knees up to her chest, and calmly guided Serena with the contractions, he could see the head of the first baby.

'Come on Serena love, just push the baby out now, one big lurch!' She screamed out and the baby girl slid out. He grabbed hold of the baby and instructed Jacqueline to bring the towels over, she was crying out loud! He placed her in Jacqueline's arms for a moment, as the second baby was just behind....

Serena began to cry and spoke,

'I cannot push anymore; I cannot do this'

Jason, calmly said to her,

'You can Serena, you just need to breathe in and out slowly, just so slowly get your rhythm going, slowly, slowly, she was being hypnotised by Jason, she was almost falling asleep, and he shouted. Now! Serena, now! push, push, we are nearly there come on girl, you can do it'

Serena pushed her heart out, and out popped the boy, he was crying loudly... Dylan, holding Serena's hand as the boy was placed on her chest. The doorbell rang, Jacqueline opened it and there stood Mr Sanders.

He entered the room and checked on Serena and turned to Jason.

'Well Jason, are you sure you are in the right field at the hospital? You might want to switch to Obstetrics. You have done a fine job. We will get you all to hospital, the ambulance was behind me. You can have a lovely rest, Serena; you look like you need it.

Jason and Jacqueline sat in the kitchen having a well-deserved cup of tea.

'You were absolutely amazing Jason; I cannot believe what has just happened,' said Jacqueline.

Jason's adrenaline had kicked in, and he was overwhelmed a little and he too was taken back at the events that had just happened. The babies were a good size he thought.

They both sat down together, a little exhausted. Jacqueline put her hand in Jason's hand,

'Let's not venture out to the busy Christmas Fayre, I can rustle something special up at my cottage, what say you, my dear?'

Jason kissed her passionately…

'I take it, that's a yes then', as Jacqueline quivered with delight…

They eventually arrived back at the cottage and talked of Christmas, and Jacqueline wanted all her family to be together but now there were additions to the family, she hadn't got the room she wanted. Jason came up with a plan, it was a good plan.

He began telling Jacqueline that when his father was alive, he used the outbuilding for Christmas barn dances and big get togethers, it was all closed off, all the furniture and fixtures were covered with sheets, it would just need brushing up a bit and everyone could come along.

Jacqueline began thinking of Emily and Frankie and his family.

'What about Jack and is family too', Niamh would love that', as Jacqueline murmured away. All our families come to think of it. This sounded a great idea.

Jason looked om with admiration….

It was settled she would spring it on everyone. As they sat enjoying a light lunch, Niamh entered room. She thought the idea was great, to have all the families together.

Emily was more than happy to come along as she wanted to know more about this Mr Charleston.

The following week Jason set about getting the outbuilding ready for the big Christmas Day ahead. The annexe adjacent to the barn had four bedrooms which hadn't been used for years. He was hoping Mrs Biggins would contribute to the extra cleaning. He would give her a generous Christmas bonus. She was more than happy to help.

Colm and Emily were of the same view; this relationship their mam was having with Mr Charleston was happening too quickly for them. It was Niamh who was the settled one, as she felt that her mam sparkled around Jason. She loved her dad dearly, but she knew he would be happy for her, she felt that.

Jacqueline attended mass on Christmas Day and gave her warm wishes to Fr Donnelly, who couldn't help but notice Jacqueline's happy eyes, he hadn't seen them like that since Declan was alive. He greeted Jacqueline with a lovely gesture.

'Happy Christmas, be happy, you deserve to be happy'

The day was a delightful success, and Jason had put on a Christmas Day to remember.

The room was fully decorated with a glorious big tree in the corner. He had gone to town and got all manufacturers in. He had even invested in a professional chef to do the whole days food and drink.

Everyone, toasted Jason for a fantastic Christmas day. Emily was overcome with it all and after having a few glasses of wine she approached Jason and asked him his intentions towards her mam.

Jason stood back a little rather surprised at Emily directness.

'My intentions Emily are to make your mam very happy,' said he

'What do you mean by very happy, be more specific please,' said Emily

'I love your mam, and I hope one day I will ask for her hand, I would ask the families permission first, I think that is the proper way to go about it,' said he

Emily stunned by such a response stood a moment, a good few moments and replied

'I see, well, thank you for that', as she walked back to her seat...

That very night, Emily sat outside with her sister Niamh, as they all stayed at Jasons...

They watched the stars come out as they sat outside his stables, pondering their mam's future...

'Mam, has been on such a journey, since our dad died, the pain and sadness was so great, and now her life has become so joyful, and she deserves that'

Niamh sprang into action and grabbed two wine glasses and a bottle of Chardonnay and spoke out with such passion in her voice.

'To mam and Jason, may they be happy ever after'

Emily further went on to say,

'I will drink to that'

They both went inside and said their goodnights.

Jason and Jacqueline were locked in their own little world upstairs… ….

www.ingramcontent.com/pod-product-compliance
Lightning Source LLC
Chambersburg PA
CBHW070406120526
44590CB00014B/1277